Moving C

# Computer Basics

*Improve your skills and get more from your computer*

**CAROL DOLMAN**
**and**
**MARCUS SAUNDERS**

| NOTTINGHAMSHIRE COUNTY COUNCIL | |
|---|---|
| H J | |
| 004.16 | £9.99 |
| | |

**How To Books**

Published by How To Books Ltd, 3 Newtec Place,
Magdalen Road, Oxford OX4 1RE. United Kingdom.
Tel: (01865) 793806. Fax: (01865) 248780.
email: info@howtobooks.co.uk
www.howtobooks.co.uk

All rights reserved. No part of this work may be reproduced
or stored in an information retrieval system (other than for
purposes of review) without the express permission of the
publisher in writing.

© **Copyright 2000 Carol Dolman and Marcus Saunders**

British Library Cataloguing in Publication Data.
A catalogue record for this book is available from
the British Library.

Edited by Julie Nelson
Cover design by Shireen Nathoo Design
Cover image PhotoDisc

Produced for How To Books by Deer Park Productions
Typeset by PDQ Typesetting, Newcastle-under-Lyme, Staffs.
Printed and bound by Cromwell Press, Trowbridge, Wiltshire

NOTE: The material contained in this book is set out in good
faith for general guidance and no liability can be accepted
for loss or expense incurred as a result of relying in particular
circumstances on statements made in the book. Laws and
regulations are complex and liable to change, and readers should
check the current position with the relevant authorities before
making personal arrangements.

# Contents

| | |
|---|---|
| **List of Illustrations** | **8** |
| **Preface** | **11** |

**1 Looking deeper into Windows' menus** — **13**
  Exploring the control panel — 13
  Installing and viewing fonts — 20
  Discovering other useful functions — 22
  Entertainment with Windows' world of multimedia — 24
  Sharing information with direct cable connection — 27
  Case study — 31
  Practical exercise — 31

**2 Fulfilment with photograph editing** — **34**
  Purchases that will improve ability — 34
  Getting a photograph into the computer — 36
  Manipulation techniques and their uses — 40
  Some other ideas of practical uses — 45
  Case study — 46
  Practical exercise — 47

**3 Making a word processor work more effectively** — **48**
  Constructing the layout with columns and tables — 48
  Creating and placing drawings and pictures — 52
  Manipulating tabs, bullets and numbering — 55
  Exploring voice dictation, OCR scanning and macros — 58
  Explaining file conversion for importing/exporting — 61
  Case study — 63
  Practical exercise — 63

| | | |
|---|---|---|
| **4** | **Enhancing the work of spreadsheets** | **66** |
| | Making your worksheet more attractive | 66 |
| | Creating a chart from a table | 72 |
| | Setting the print requirements | 74 |
| | An introduction to using controls | 75 |
| | Case study | 80 |
| **5** | **Home accounting with finance packages** | **81** |
| | Using a finance program | 81 |
| | Setting up a money program | 82 |
| | Keeping your finances up to date | 85 |
| | Making the accounts balance | 87 |
| | More effective money managers | 89 |
| | Summary | 90 |
| | Case study | 90 |
| **6** | **Dealing with databases** | **91** |
| | The dilemma of databases | 91 |
| | Creating a database using the wizard | 93 |
| | Using reports and picking out records | 97 |
| | Producing labels from selected records | 99 |
| | Saving time with mail merge | 100 |
| | Case study | 102 |
| **7** | **More wonders of the web** | **103** |
| | Connecting to the Internet | 103 |
| | Finding what you are looking for | 105 |
| | Downloading from the Internet | 109 |
| | Building and publishing a web page | 112 |
| | Case study | 117 |
| | Practical exercise | 118 |
| **8** | **Essential program utilities to consider** | **120** |
| | Keeping your files secret with security programs | 120 |
| | Creating and unzipping compressed files | 122 |
| | The advantages of CD writers and Zip drives | 127 |
| | Creating partitions and disk imaging | 129 |
| | Case study | 132 |

| | | |
|---|---|---|
| **9** | **Making use of communication resources** | 134 |
| | Networking two computers together | 134 |
| | Connecting to another local computer | 138 |
| | Linking to remote computers | 140 |
| | Case study | 144 |
| | | |
| **10** | **When things start to go wrong** | 145 |
| | Saving yourself some frustration | 145 |
| | Diagnosing where the blame lies | 146 |
| | Common problems you may come across | 148 |
| | Resolving problems | 150 |
| | It's not always the fault of the obvious | 154 |
| | Summary | 159 |

| | |
|---|---|
| Appendix: Recommended software and hardware purchases | 160 |
| Glossary | 163 |
| Further Reading | 169 |
| Index | 171 |

# List of Illustrations

| | | |
|---|---|---|
| 1 | A typical Control Panel | 14 |
| 2 | The Add/Remove programs properties box | 14 |
| 3 | The Windows Setup properties box | 15 |
| 4 | The Add New Hardware wizard | 17 |
| 5 | The Keyboard properties box | 18 |
| 6 | The magnifier tool | 19 |
| 7 | Viewing an individual font | 20 |
| 8 | Viewing the fonts folder | 21 |
| 9 | The Find Files dialogue box | 23 |
| 10 | A typical Windows menu system | 24 |
| 11 | The Media Player dialogue box | 25 |
| 12 | The ActiveMovie control box | 25 |
| 13 | The CD Player control box | 27 |
| 14 | CD Player track labelling box | 27 |
| 15 | DCC host or guest wizard | 28 |
| 16 | The Network properties box | 29 |
| 17 | The sharing properties box | 30 |
| 18 | The waiting status of DCC | 30 |
| 19 | The Sound Recorder control box | 32 |
| 20 | The Sounds properties box | 32 |
| 21 | The Paint Shop Pro Window | 35 |
| 22 | The window of a typical scanner program | 37 |
| 23 | Showing the difference in dpi resolution | 39 |
| 24 | Clever tricks with manipulation | 40 |
| 25 | Manipulation tool icons | 41 |
| 26 | Changing selections with control palette | 42 |
| 27 | The wonders of cloning | 43 |
| 28 | Removing an eyesore | 44 |
| 29 | Setting the brush sizes | 45 |
| 30 | Various filters applied to a drawing | 47 |
| 31 | Different column layouts | 49 |
| 32 | Different ways of selecting columns | 50 |
| 33 | Inserting a table from the toolbar | 51 |
| 34 | Showing multiple and a single column | 51 |
| 35 | Creating space for easy reading | 52 |
| 36 | Grouping multiple objects together | 53 |

| | | |
|---|---|---|
| 37 | Different wrap settings | 54 |
| 38 | Different tab settings | 55 |
| 39 | Tab setting on the ruler | 56 |
| 40 | Toolbar icons for various indents | 57 |
| 41 | Getting ready to record a macro | 59 |
| 42 | The macro recording screen | 61 |
| 43 | Saving a file in a particular format | 62 |
| 44 | Some sample text | 64 |
| 45 | Have you saved the three files correctly? | 65 |
| 46 | Altering the width of columns | 67 |
| 47 | Merging cells and centring text | 68 |
| 48 | Adding borders | 69 |
| 49 | The border formatting box | 69 |
| 50 | Using the fill series | 70 |
| 51 | Toolbar icons for information order | 71 |
| 52 | The autoformat dialogue box | 72 |
| 53 | The chart wizard | 72 |
| 54 | A finished table and chart | 73 |
| 55 | The print area options | 74 |
| 56 | Some sample text | 76 |
| 57 | How your chart may look | 76 |
| 58 | Placing and formatting combo boxes | 77 |
| 59 | The finished result | 79 |
| 60 | Choosing an account to set up | 82 |
| 61 | The regular transaction boxes | 83 |
| 62 | Forward planning a transaction | 84 |
| 63 | Creating a new category | 84 |
| 64 | Paying money to another account | 86 |
| 65 | Reconciling with a statement | 87 |
| 66 | A graphical display of spending habits | 89 |
| 67 | Additional fields data | 94 |
| 68 | Personalising additional fields | 94 |
| 69 | An address book database screen | 95 |
| 70 | Toolbar icons | 95 |
| 71 | The more stylish appearance | 96 |
| 72 | Changing the tab order | 97 |
| 73 | Entering filter criteria | 98 |
| 74 | A display of records – some marked | 99 |
| 75 | Setting up address labels | 100 |
| 76 | Using database fields in mail merge | 101 |
| 77 | The finished results of a mail merge | 102 |
| 78 | The dial-up connection box | 104 |
| 79 | The address bar | 105 |

| | | |
|---|---|---|
| 80 | Selecting a search engine | 107 |
| 81 | Grabbing a picture | 110 |
| 82 | A download site | 111 |
| 83 | Setting the page size | 113 |
| 84 | Keeping frames apart | 114 |
| 85 | Creating a hyperlink | 115 |
| 86 | Checking for design faults | 116 |
| 87 | Norton's Control Centre | 121 |
| 88 | Menus for manual and automatic encryption | 121 |
| 89 | Looking inside a zipped file | 124 |
| 90 | Creating a zipped file | 124 |
| 91 | Adding files to a zip | 124 |
| 92 | Extracting from a zipped file | 125 |
| 93 | A Windows warning | 126 |
| 94 | Viewing partitions and drives | 129 |
| 95 | The network configuration box | 136 |
| 96 | Allowing file and print sharing | 137 |
| 97 | The Network Neighbourhood screen | 138 |
| 98 | Mapping a drive | 139 |
| 99 | Windows remote Dial Up Networking | 141 |
| 100 | Norton PC Anywhere dial-up networking | 142 |
| 101 | Security options are strongly advised | 143 |
| 102 | Common error missing file box | 146 |
| 103 | Illegal operation error box | 148 |
| 104 | Restarting the computer | 151 |
| 105 | The uninstall program shield | 152 |
| 106 | Keeping shared files | 152 |
| 107 | The effect of an incorrect printer driver | 155 |
| 108 | Reading sound configurations | 156 |
| 109 | Setting the correct keyboard | 158 |

# Preface

After a few months of owning their first computer many people find that the novelty of loading and playing with every program they can get their hands on has worn a bit thin. If this is you, then you will probably want to justify the expense you incurred when you bought your machine and start to make it earn its keep. The computer is without doubt a wonderful invention, but how can you learn to utilise it effectively without spending all your time on it?

You have already taken the first step by choosing this book. We will now show you some of the more interesting projects that really do begin to stretch the power of your computer. You will learn what some of those extra titles in your menu system are and how they are used, plus you will gain a fuller knowledge of some of the wonderful jargon being banded about and when you may be able to use it to your advantage.

You will no doubt have experienced a few problems already such as your computer getting stroppy and refusing to do anything you ask, or scary messages appearing on the screen that appear to threaten total self-destruction. Occasionally you will do everything right and things still don't go according to plan. Don't worry, help is at hand – by the time you have read this book you should be able to tell the difference between a serious problem and a quaint characteristic.

This book is not a complete authority on computers, indeed no book is or ever could be. What you will gain from reading it is a deeper understanding so that you can progress to the level that suits you best. You will gain a broad overview of computers at work and enough knowledge to know which areas, if any, you wish to pursue in greater depth.

So now read on and cut through the hype and clutter to see what's really sitting on your desk.

*Carol Dolman and Marcus Saunders*

# 1

## Looking Deeper Into Windows' Menus

The primary function of Windows is to provide the computer user with a friendly and stable operating system and by and large it does this very well. It also, however, contains many other features, which enable us to perform a variety of tasks. Indeed many programs that you will install utilise certain aspects of Windows routines and codes, without which they wouldn't work at all.

Windows has several utilities built in which enable you to perform some basic work and listed below are some that you are no doubt familiar with by now:

- **Wordpad** – a basic but useful word processor
- **Paint** – a simple drawing package
- **Games** – those time-passing Solitaire and Minesweeper programs
- **Internet Explorer** – the browser for viewing the Internet
- **System Tools** – for monitoring and cleaning up your computer
- **Calculator** – for helping when the mind goes blank!

Some of the other additional features give us a degree of control over programs for communications, multimedia and entertainment. **Control Panel**, found in the Start menu under Settings, gives us access to many of these features. In this chapter we will look at some of these, explain what they do and how you may be able to put them to use.

### EXPLORING THE CONTROL PANEL

Figure 1 shows how a typical Control Panel window may appear when selected from the Settings menu of Windows 98. There may be some differences between this one and your own. Some programs install additional features here such as the **Find Fast** icon – this is commonly found when the computer has Microsoft Office installed. It also depends on your original Windows installation configuration as to what has been installed and is therefore available.

**14** Moving On from Computer Basics

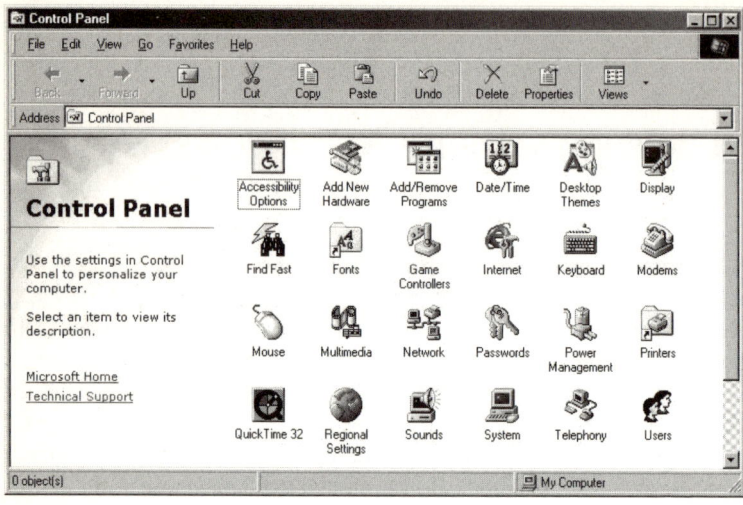

Fig. 1. A typical Control Panel.

### The importance of the Add/Remove Programs icon
This icon allows you to perform three tasks:

1. install and remove programs that use the Windows version of Install Shield
2. install and remove the Windows setup components
3. create a bootable startup disk for emergencies.

### Installing and removing programs
Windows will list a program in the **Install/Uninstall** tab if that program installs itself correctly and includes an uninstall program that is compatible with Install Shield. These programs often have the *Compatible with Windows 98* logo displayed on the box. If a program uses the **autorun** file, i.e. it automatically begins installation when the CD is inserted, but is compliant, it will still be listed in this list box. An example of the Add/Remove Programs list can be seen in Figure 2.

If either this method or the

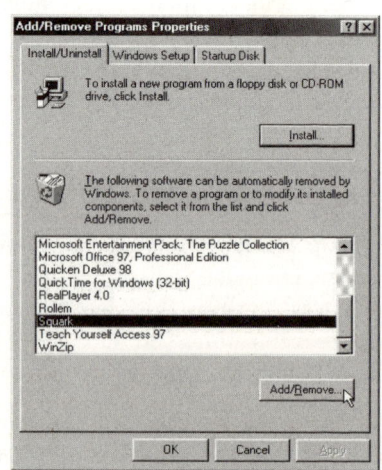

Fig. 2. The Add/Remove Programs properties box.

program's own uninstall program is used, the components that were installed initially should all be removed successfully, eliminating stray files and unnecessary clogging up of Windows registry files with redundant information.

When removing programs, there are two things to bear in mind:

1. If the uninstall shield tells you there is a shared file – do you want to remove it? Say **No**. The amount of space these shared files take up is minimal. The program may advise you that it is safe to remove it, but if another one uses it, that program may not run if the shared file is uninstalled.

2. Once a program has uninstalled, go into **Explorer** and check that the parent folder for the program has also been removed. The uninstall program may have left some files, such as saved game or user profile type files. If the parent folder is still there, right click it and hit delete – removing any last traces to avoid possible confusion later.

### Installing and removing Windows components

During some installations of Windows, you will be given a choice as to whether or not you wish to install certain components. If you have chosen the Custom installation, this list will be quite large. If someone else installed Windows for you, or you chose the Typical button, then you may wish to install some of the components omitted at a later date. You do this from the Windows Setup tab of Add/Remove Programs.

When you click on the tab it displays items in categories; for example, the **Accessories** tab includes components such as **Notepad**, **Calculator** and **Wallpapers**.

- The boxes that display a tick already have that component installed.
- To uninstall a component, uncheck the box.
- Blank boxes can be checked to install items.
- A box appears greyed with a tick if only partial elements of that category are installed.
- Click on **Details** to display which elements of that category are installed as seen in Figure 3.

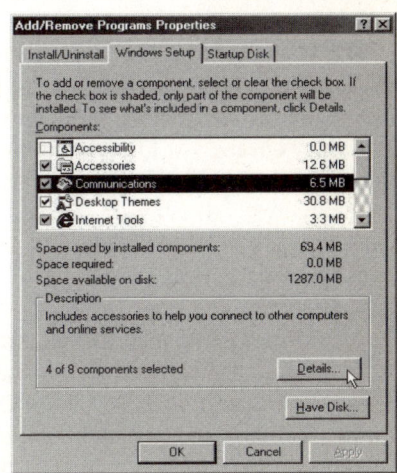

Fig. 3. The Windows Setup properties box.

*I wanted to install something, but it says I already have it installed!*
Windows allows the computer to be set up for multiple users and each user can set up the desktop for the way they like to work. This is known as a **user profile**. If a user installs an element such as **Desktop Themes**, then although it is on the computer, it may not be available to other users, because it is stored in the user profile of the person who installed it.

For another user to be able to access this component, they will have to uncheck the box and click **Apply** – thus uninstalling the component – then re-check it and click **Apply** again. It will then be available to the second user as well as the first.

### Creating a bootable startup disk
The startup disk provides a way of booting up a computer without using the installed operating system. It is most commonly used when files on the hard disk have become corrupted, stopping the computer from booting properly. It is wise to create one of these and label it accordingly then place it somewhere safe – you never know when you may need it. You need one blank floppy disk onto which you can copy the Windows startup files. If you do not use it yourself, it may be useful to an engineer who finds himself sorting a problem out for you, saving him time and you money.

### Using the Add New Hardware icon
A lot of new hardware is plug and play compatible, in which case Windows will automatically install the drivers required – or at least make an attempt to look for them and then prompt you to insert the manufacturer's disk containing these drivers if it cannot find them.

When Windows cannot, for some reason, detect your new hardware or the item being fitted is not plug and play, the **Add New Hardware** icon can be used to initialise the installation. The wizard will run through its necessary checks just to make sure it isn't plug and play. The choices then, as seen in Figure 4, are to give Windows the opportunity to attempt to automatically detect your installed hardware or to just go ahead and install the new drivers by pointing it toward an installation disk from the manufacturer.

### Personalising the way things are set up
Many of the icons in Control Panel can be used to change the way your system and attachments are set up. The **Date/Time** icon, for example, shows what time and day your computer thinks it is. If these are all set up properly, the spring and autumn clock changes of an hour back and forth will adjust accordingly.

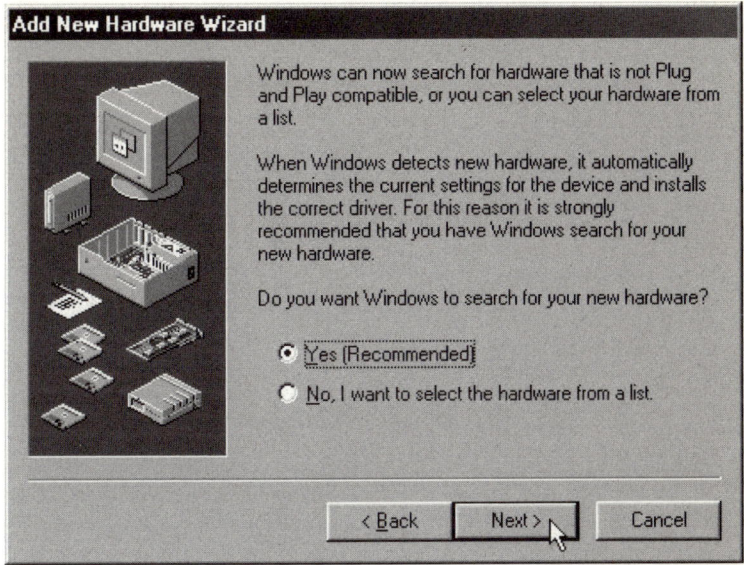

Fig. 4. The Add New Hardware wizard.

If you run any programs such as Flight Simulator which enable you to fly during 'real' time, the computer will reflect this from these settings – if you begin your flight just before dusk, it will get darker as you fly. Some screensavers will use these settings to reflect the time of day – in daylight they will display daylight scenes and in the dark evenings, a night-time scene.

### In what language do you type?

The **Keyboard** icon enables you to plug in different keyboards for different languages – ideal if you are a foreign language teacher or student who has to type essays. A German keyboard that is plugged in with the driver installed as seen in Figure 5 will automatically put all those little umlauts in the right places. This needs to be set to an English British keyboard for us – if the default installation has left it at English American, you may find the pound sign puts the # mark instead, as well as other differences. The Keyboard icon also allows you to change the speed at which the keys respond to you pressing them and the rate at which the cursor flashes on the screen.

### Giving those with disabilities a helping hand

The **Accessibility** option can be installed from the Windows Setup tab of Add/Remove Programs. Once installed, it provides tools that change

**18** Moving On from Computer Basics

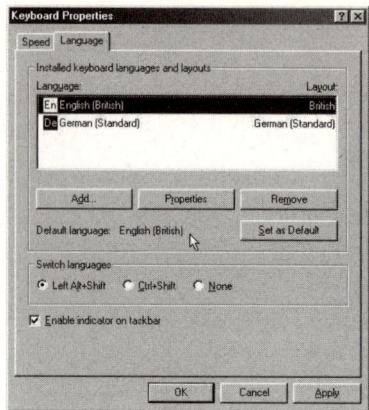

Fig. 5. The Keyboard Properties box.

keyboard, sound, display and mouse behaviour for people with mobility, hearing or visual impairments.

Click on the icon in the Control Panel to see the dialogue box that allows you to set up various features. For example, on the first tab – Keyboard – people who find combined keystrokes hard to use, such as holding down the shift key with a letter to produce a capital, may find the **StickyKeys** useful. With this turned on, a small symbol resembling three keys appears on the Taskbar. When the operation is required, just press the first key, i.e. the shift – this lights up one of the keys on the symbol showing that key is still active. Then press the other letter and a capital will appear. Pressing the two keys together in the normal way turns the feature off.

In the **Mouse** section, the number pad on your keyboard can be configured to control the mouse pointer on your screen. The **Sound** tab can be used to generate visual warnings when your system makes a sound. The **Display** tab lets you choose from the Windows colour schemes and font settings that are highly contrasted and therefore easier to see than the standard ones. Finally, the **General** tab has an option to set up other specialist devices that you may want to attach to your PC instead of a mouse or keyboard.

*Magnifying your path*
By pointing to the Accessibility option in the Start menus, not from the Control Panel, you can switch on the **magnifier tool**. This generates a spare inch or two at the top of your screen to magnify wherever your mouse is going as seen in Figure 6. This will be applied to any program that is running.

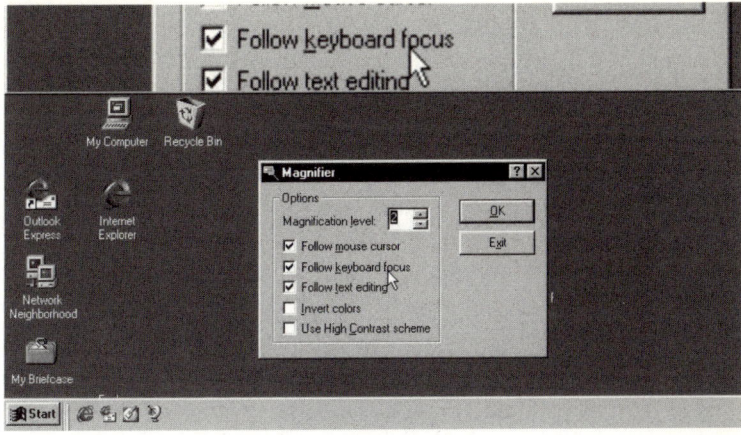

Fig. 6. The magnifier tool.

## Some of the remaining options in brief

- **The Display icon** – gives access to the setting up of screensavers, wallpapers, screen resolution and appearances, plus effects that can be produced with desktop icons.

- **Desktop Themes** – if installed, turns your desktop, mouse cursor, folders, sounds and screensavers into a theme. For example, with Dangerous Creatures, the wallpaper is of a beautiful lion, the desktop icons folders are changed to various animals, the mouse cursor becomes a bee and sounds resemble noises from the jungle.

- **Regional Settings** – ensures dates are displayed in the correct format and that normal measurements and currency settings are used for the country you are located in. As with the keyboard, you will need to set these for UK Greenwich Mean Time, as the default setting is for America.

- **Users** – enables individual desktop settings to be profiled for particular users. Each user can then log on using their own password and will see their customised setting such as wallpaper and desktop icons in view.

**20** Moving On from Computer Basics

- **Mouse** – change it from being right-handed to being a left-handed mouse. Alter the appearance of the cursors and the motion that displays its trail.

- **Sounds** – lists all of the sounds used during Windows operations. Try a different scheme or change whether a specific sound occurs at a certain time. Additional sample sounds can be installed from the Windows Setup tab as described earlier, or you can record your own.

- **Power Management** – control of when your computer shuts down particular resources after a period of inactivity, such as the monitor and hard drive. Some computers have power management in their BIOS as well. If you find your computer locks up when you try to revive it after a period of inactivity, turn off one of the power saving features, preferably the one in the BIOS, as this will probably be conflicting with the Windows management.

- **Game Controllers** – used to configure and calibrate game controllers such as joysticks.

- **Internet** – holds all the information on Internet connection setups. Home pages, telephone numbers and cache settings can be found and configured from here.

## INSTALLING AND VIEWING FONTS

A **font** is a set of character shapes of a certain size, weight, style and design that together make up a **typeface** – letters that you type. Windows installs quite a few, as do some programs such as Microsoft Publisher. You can buy additional fonts or install them from demo and shareware disks and download them from the Internet. Catalogue programs are available for viewing and printing out fonts and these enable you to see at a glance the range available to you.

Fig. 7. Viewing an individual font.

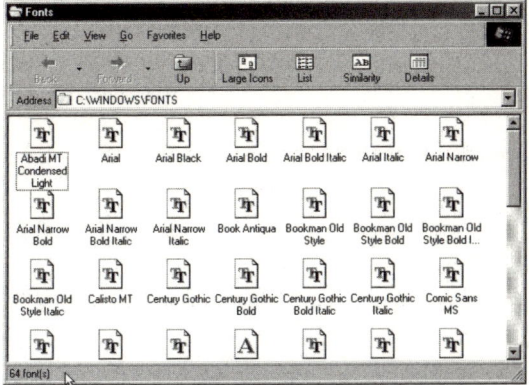

Fig. 8. Viewing the fonts folder.

The **font folder** in the Control Panel holds installed fonts. Double clicking on any one will display a box showing the style of the font selected in varying sizes as seen in Figure 7. A sample of it can also be printed from here. Any font that is installed using the **Install New Font** command from the file menu should also be available in other programs, such as word processors, when the font drop-down box is selected.

### Limiting the number of fonts installed

Every time Windows starts up, it loads each and every font that is installed in the Windows\Fonts folder. Equally, every time the font drop-down list box is selected in a program application, these fonts are read and displayed. For this reason, the amount of fonts installed here should be limited. The maximum Windows can cope with is around 1,000 because of the limits to the listing of them in the Registry. A much more realistic figure so as not to grind your system to a halt may be around 250. The amount you have installed is shown at the bottom of the folder window as shown in Figure 8, if the Status Bar option is checked in the View menu.

### Handling fonts if you use a lot of them

The best way is to purchase a font viewer and either leave fonts on a disk or copy them into a separate folder on your hard drive to view them, then install them only when they are required. Do not be tempted to try installing all of those 10,000 fonts you have just purchased for a few pounds – it would cause you more problems than it is worth!

## DISCOVERING OTHER USEFUL FUNCTIONS

### Traits of your taskbar

The Windows 98 taskbar – the long strip usually found along the bottom of your screen that contains the Start button – can be customised to your own tastes. Firstly, it can be moved to any other side of the screen simply by dragging it with the mouse pointer placed in any spare space of the bar. Secondly, if you click the **Start** button, point to **Settings** and then **Taskbar**, you can alter the information that it displays and the way it reacts when applications are launched. For example, it can always stay on top, which means it will always be in view, or it can **Auto-hide**. Auto-hide means it will not be in view until you need it. To call it back, place your mouse pointer over the edge where the bar should be, and it will re-appear.

Additional toolbars can be added to the taskbar by right-clicking in a blank area of the bar and choosing **new toolbar**. Navigate your way to the folder you wish to assign as a toolbar. The new toolbar, complete with any files that are in the chosen folder, can now be accessed from the taskbar, or can be dragged off the taskbar as a separate toolbar on the desktop.

### Accessing and clearing recently used files

All documents opened recently are logged in the Documents list just off the Start menu. Clicking on a file here opens the file along with its necessary application such as the word processor that created it. This makes it easy to access documents, but can have its drawbacks by showing everyone else who uses the computer what you have been working on.

To clear this, select the **Start Menu Programs** tab from the **Taskbar Properties** and click on the **Clear** button. The list will now appear empty again.

### Finding lost or misplaced files

If you cannot find a file that you know is on your hard drive somewhere, the **Find** command off the **Start** menu can help. In our example, a piece of homework was created about acid rainwater. We know that it was saved with the words geography-something. We placed asterisks in the areas where there may be other letters or words. Also, to enhance our search, we knew there were no other documents with the words acid rainwater in them, so we entered that as text which is contained within the document (Windows 95 does not have this option). Figure 9 shows how these details were entered and where the document was found hiding.

- Type in the name of your file, using an asterisk for any missing words.
- If you are not sure of the file's extension, use a wildcard, i.e. an asterisk replaces any name.
- Ensure that the root of your hard drive is selected in the **Look in:** field.
- Check the **Include subfolders** box to maximise your search.
- Click on **Find Now**. If your file is on your hard drive, it will be found in seconds.

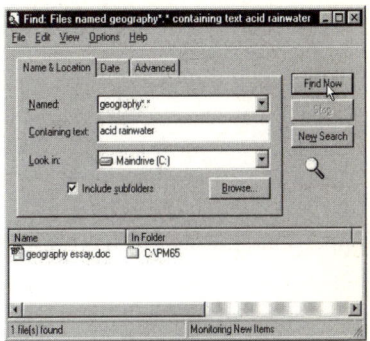

Fig. 9. The Find Files dialogue box.

### Backing up your files with Windows 98 Backup

Windows 95 Backup was quite useful but this has much improved with Windows 98. There are more options and it is quick and easy to use. If you have a lot of large, important files that you need to back up regularly, it may be worth investing in a more secure way of backing up, such as a removable disk or tape drive. However, if the data you are backing up is not vital and you just wish to give yourself a chance of being able to restore it if something terrible happens to your system, then you can use Backup. It can be found in the System Tools menu. It is not installed by default so you may have to go to the Windows Setup tab and install it first.

*How does Backup work?*
Backup creates one file that will contain a compressed version of all the selected files previously chosen to be backed up. This can then be saved to another media, such as another hard drive partition or floppy disks. Should an accident happen that causes you to lose those files, they can be restored from this location once your computer is up and running again.

*Does it take very long?*
This depends on what you choose to back up. It can be used to back up full programs, but this will often result in needing many blank floppy disks and a lot of spare time. Its common use is to back up files that you have created yourself, such as your word processing documents. If you get into good habits of storing all your own files in one particular folder, such as the My Documents folder, Backup is an easy task to complete and should not take very long at all.

The first time Backup is run, a job is created – taking the above example, the job would be to back up all files in the My Documents folder. The job is created by identifying a backup file name and selecting the files to be added. Files are selected by ticking the indicator boxes next to the folders. Once this has been created, a further job can be set up and named something like Update. This job's task would be adding new files and updating any changed files that appear in the My Documents folder since the last backup file was stored.

*Restoring lost files after a computer hiccup*
Once your computer is up and running again, Backup can be run but this time selecting the **Restore** option. All files that were backed up will be restored onto the computer and you will be back in action again.

There are many other ways of backing up and protecting files, some of which are discussed in Chapter 8.

## ENTERTAINMENT WITH WINDOWS' WORLD OF MULTIMEDIA

In the Entertainment menu as seen in Figure 10 there are a few programs enabling the recording and playing of sound clips and video. Again, these have quite basic facilities and if you intend to use a computer for professional sound recording or video editing, there are additional programs available that offer much more flexibility and control.

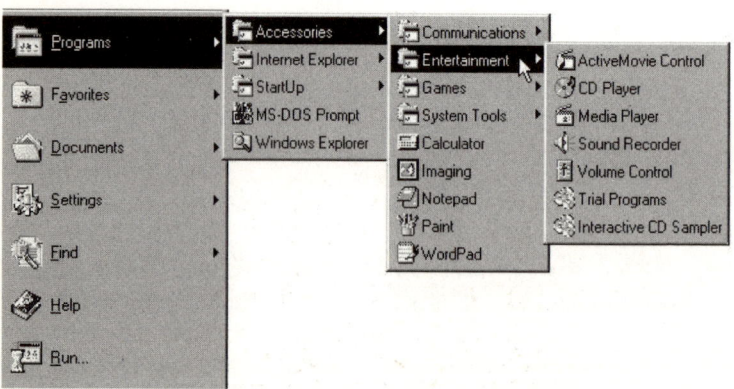

Fig. 10. A typical Windows menu system.

### Film viewing with Media Player or ActiveMovie Control

You can use Media Player to play audio, video or animation files and to control the settings for multimedia hardware devices. Click on the File menu to open the relevant file and Media Player will begin playing it. In Figure 11 we had a sample of Beethoven's Fifth Symphony in the Windows/Media folder. This is one of the sample sounds installed from Windows 98. The controls at the bottom of the dialogue box are similar to those of a cassette deck. You can play, stop, forward and rewind your clip.

Fig. 11. The Media Player dialogue box.

The movies can be animated as we show in Figure 12 or an actual piece of film such as a panther sprinting across safari land. Figure 12 is an animated picture that an encyclopaedia has put together to explain how radio beacons transmit their signals to the player in a home. The video clip has a voice explaining what is happening at the same time as you can see the operator turning the controls on, and the radio waves transmitting to the machine. Again you have the play, pause and stop controls at the bottom, plus an indicator bar of how long the movie is. Many multimedia encyclopaedias use a similar window when you select various topics.

Fig. 12. The ActiveMovie control box.

### Recording with the Sound Recorder

Sound Recorder can be used to record, play and edit sound files. To record sounds, you will need a microphone. Again there are controls to play, record, stop, forward and rewind. In the window you see a graph to represent your sound. Special effects can be added, such as echo or increased volume, then played back. The newly recorded sound files can be saved and used in the Windows sound scheme or other programs such as an outgoing message for your computer answerphone. Check out the practical exercise at the end of this chapter.

### Viewing the Interactive CD Sampler

The Interactive CD Sampler requires the Windows CD to be in the CD-ROM. You can install the whole thing for viewing or do a temporary installation. The latter is suggested, as the likelihood of viewing this more than once is very remote – once seen never forgotten! It is basically an advert for other Microsoft computer products that are available. The program allows you to choose which area of life you are interested in using your computer for, such as learning, working, etc. and will go on to show you products that may help you in that area.

### Trying out trial programs

This is again an advert for Microsoft products but has the advantage this time of having trial versions of particular programs for you to try. Select the programs you would like to try by checking the box. Trial versions will have varying limitations as to their use. For example, there may be a time-limited trial of 30 days, or with a product such as Arcade Games you will only be given one of the games to try out.

### Music while you work

You can use **CD Player** to play audio compact disks on your computer's CD-ROM while you work. Headphones can be used – they normally plug in at the front of the CD-ROM – or the speaker system of your computer.

As soon as you put a music CD into the drive, the CD Player will display as shown in Figure 13. If it doesn't, select it from the Entertainment menu. If it is not installed, see 'Installing and removing Windows components' earlier in this chapter. Use the controls as you would on a hi-fi system. The titles of the tracks can be entered into the database so that this is included in the display. From the Disc menu select **Edit Play List**. The boxes enable you to enter the artist and individual tracks by selecting the track number and changing the text in the bottom box to that of the title as shown in Figure 14.

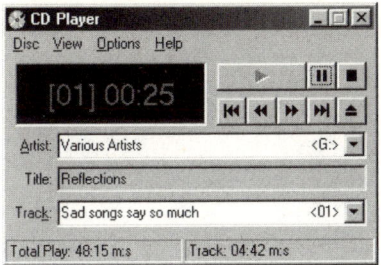

Fig. 13. The CD Player control box.

If the music volume needs adjustment and there are no volume controls on your speakers, the **Volume Control** from the Entertainment menu can be used to adjust it accordingly.

Fig. 14. CD Player track labelling box.

## SHARING INFORMATION WITH DIRECT CABLE CONNECTION

Direct cable connection (DCC) is one of the Windows utilities found in the Communications menu when installed. It is not installed with a typical installation, so you may have to use the Windows Setup tab in Add/Remove Programs of Control Panel to install it. Select **Communications** and check mark the **DCC box**. The Dial Up Networking will have to be installed as well in order to configure the network protocols necessary to run DCC, but Windows will tell you this at the time.

### What is DCC (Direct Cable Connection)?

Simply put, it is a way of connecting two computers together. One is set up as a **host**, the other as a **guest**, as seen in Figure 15. Providing the host computer has been configured to share some of its folders or drives, the guest computer can connect to it and use files and drives from the host as if it was one of its own. It is a sort of network, without the need for a network card inside the computer and a possibly complicated setup procedure. This should not be considered an alternative to a network where permanent or semi-permanent connections are necessary.

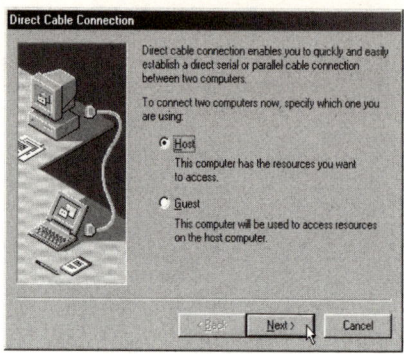

Fig. 15. DCC host or guest wizard.

*When would I use it?*
People can often find themselves with two computers. It may be that when you bought a fast new machine, you kept the old one just in case the new one went wrong. You may have one of your own and another family member may have their own. Then of course the obvious – you may have a laptop and a desktop to fulfil your computing needs while on the road.

### The valuable uses of direct cable connection

- It enables the transfer of files from one computer to another.
- It is ideal for backing up files onto another machine in case of breakdown.
- It takes away the need to compress larger files to fit onto floppy disks.
- The guest computer can run programs and use drives from the host computer.
- Useful if the old computer had a program that you no longer have the disks for.
- If one computer doesn't have a CD-ROM it can use the resource of the other computer.
- It's cheap.

All you need to run DCC is a **null modem cable** – otherwise known as a **Laplink cable**. These can be purchased for a few pounds at Dixons, Tandy or any other computer outlet. A printer cable will not work with

# Looking Deeper Into Windows Menus 29

this type of connection. Serial port cables work slower than parallel port cables, but whichever type you are using, each end is attached to the computers relevant port. Both computers need to be running either Windows 95 or 98 (they don't have to both be running the same version) and both computers need to run the direct cable connection wizard.

## Essential preparations to carry out on both computers

1. In Control Panel, select the **Network** icon to display the dialogue box (see Figure 16).

2. Ensure that both computers have the **IPX/SPX** compatible protocol showing. If they don't, click the **Add** button and install it by choosing **Protocol**, then **Microsoft** and selecting it from the list.

3. Ensure file sharing, and printer sharing if relevant, are checked on the host computer by clicking on the **File and Print Sharing** button.

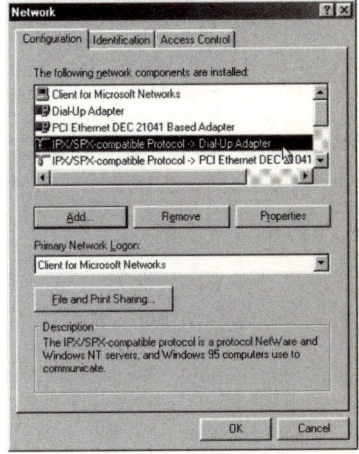

Fig. 16. The Network properties box.

4. Click on the **Identification** tab and ensure each computer has an individual name, but the same Workgroup name. A description is optional.

5. Make sure both computers have the same **Primary Network Logon** client showing.

6. After rebooting the computers, on the host machine, double click **My Computer** then right-click each drive, folder or printer you wish to share and select **Sharing** from the menu.

7. Check **Shared As** and give the drive a name and any password requirements as seen in Figure 17.

## Setting up the connections

To access DCC, point to Programs/Accessories/Communications and finally the direct cable connection wizard. The wizard pops up as shown in Figure 15 and helps you to configure your machine.

## 30 Moving On from Computer Basics

*Am I the Host?*
If it is your machine that is supplying the resources, i.e. your CD-ROM is going to be used by another computer or a program on your machine is going to be used by another computer, then you are the host. In addition, if the file that you wish to transfer is on this computer, you are the host.

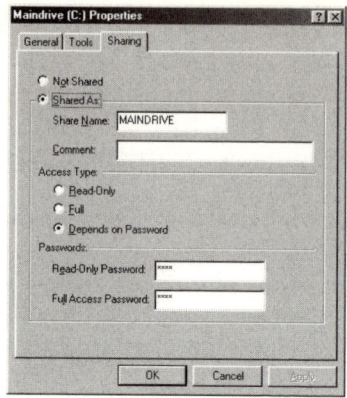

*Or am I the guest?*
If you need to use a program that is on another computer, your computer does not have a CD-ROM so

Fig. 17. The sharing properties box.

you are going to load a program from another computer's CD-ROM or the file you need is on another computer, then you are the guest.

The wizard will check out the available ports on the computer – direct it to the one you have the cable attached to then click Finish. The host computer will display the box shown in Figure 18 until the guest has connected. Once both are connected, a box will appear on the guest showing available resources from the host computer.

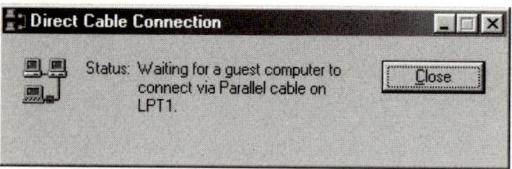

Fig. 18. The waiting status of DCC.

Installation of Direct Cable Connection puts the Network Neighbourhood icon on your desktop. Do not remove this otherwise Direct Cable Connection may not run. Network neighbourhood can be double clicked on to access the resources of a host machine – but only if the host machine's Browser Master is enabled.

*Enabling the Network Neighbourhood Browser Master*

1. On the host machine, click the Network icon in Control Panel.
2. In the Configuration panel select **File and Printer Sharing for Microsoft Networks** – this is often at the bottom of the list.

3. Click on the Properties button and turn the **Browse Master** value to **Enabled**. Click OK.

The Windows operating system is a very complex and (sometimes) clever piece of software. Although it can seem a little daunting and confusing when you begin your computing experience, it is worthwhile getting to know as much about it as you can.

Most call outs for engineers' attention are traceable to software problems rather than faults with the machine itself and so in many cases are avoidable. Knowing just that little bit more could save you money and prevent your system ending up flying out of the window in frustration.

## CASE STUDY

### Bob reclaims some much needed disk space

Bob had always tried to keep a tidy computer system by removing programs that he no longer used. Recently, however, Bob found he was running short of disk space and needed to make some room for his new software. He went through his menu system and checked for any uninstall programs that he may have missed, but found none that was of any use.

Eventually he phoned a friend who he knew had just done a computer course and asked her for any suggestions. He knew that he still had some programs on the machine that he wasn't using, but didn't know how to get rid of them if there was no uninstall entry in the menu. She explained to him about the Add/Remove programs feature in the Control Panel and how to use it.

Following the advice he was given, Bob correctly removed several programs that did not have the uninstall in the menu and recovered nearly half a gigabyte of disk space. Following a **defrag**, he also noticed that his computer was noticeably quicker in normal use.

## PRACTICAL EXERCISE

We briefly mentioned earlier the ability to record sounds. In this exercise we will take you step by step through the procedure for recording a sound. We will then show you how to attach this sound to an action that you perform within Windows. Most computers have a sound card and speakers – the only extra you will need is a microphone, costing around £10 or less.

## 32 Moving On from Computer Basics

Fig. 19. The Sound Recorder control box.

1. Go to the Entertainment menu and select **Sound Recorder**. If you do not have this option, go to the Windows Setup tab in Add/Remove Programs and install it from the Multimedia box.

2. The Sound Recorder buttons resemble those of a cassette recorder as seen in Figure 19. There is a record, stop, play forward and rewind button. The line will represent sound waves when we begin recording. With your mic to hand, press the record button and create a sound or say a few words. Press the square stop button when you have finished. For our example, we will record a very quick message saying 'bye-bye' which we will attach to closing a program.

3. Play your sound back by rewinding it and pressing the play button. If it is distorted, record it again holding the mic a little further away. If it is too quiet, from the **Effects** menu increase the volume and try it again. There are other effects in this menu that you can experiment with.

4. Once you are happy with your sound, from the file menu click on **Save**. Navigate your way to the **Windows/Media** folder which is where all other sound files are stored. Give your sound a name – we called ours Bye-Bye – and click the **Save** button.

5. To assign the sound to the closing of a program, double click on the **Sounds** icon in the Control Panel. Scroll down the **Events** list and select **Close Program**. In the **Name** box as seen in Figure 20, select the sound file that you have just created. All the sound files here are those that are in the Windows\Media folder so if yours isn't there, check where you saved it then copy and paste it into this folder.

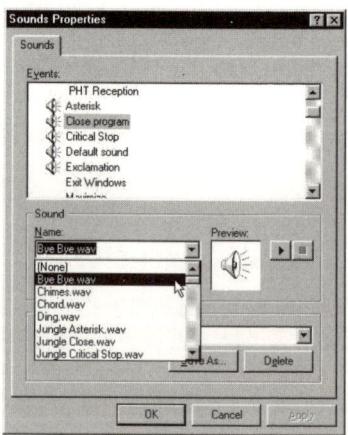

Fig. 20. The Sounds Properties box.

6. Click on the **Apply** button, then when you click on OK – which closes the Sounds dialogue box – your sound will play. Open and close another program to hear your sound again.

Your file is automatically saved in the WAV format (pronounced 'wave'). The Internet has many sound files of this format that you can download and use in the same way.

We hope that this chapter has given you a deeper insight into Windows, and a taste for some of the power it contains. The more you know about your operating system, the more control you will have over your computer.

# 2

# Fulfilment with Photograph Editing

Some things we use computers for are serious and some things are fun – photograph editing is serious fun.

## PURCHASES THAT WILL IMPROVE ABILITY

As recently as 1996 you would have had to pay out more than £3,000 to own a computer that would provide you with the power necessary to deal adequately with large graphics files such as true colour photographs. Scanners cost a lot of money and digital cameras were only just coming onto the scene with price tags that only professionals could justify and quality that they couldn't. To print out the finished product you would require a high-priced printer that was capable of achieving results that complemented the time and effort put into it. Now things have changed dramatically and playing around with photographs is one of the best bits of fun to be had on a computer.

To gain the full benefits from photograph editing you should consider purchasing the following items. These will be in addition to the computer of course, which should preferably be of mid-range power and have as much memory and hard drive space as you can afford.

### Digital Camera

These take the photographs and allow you to transfer the pictures from the camera to the computer using special downloading software that usually comes packaged with the purchase. Digital cameras work in much the same way as an ordinary camera with one important exception – they don't use film. Instead they use a special kind of disk – like a mini floppy disk – to store the pictures on. Most cameras will allow you to view the pictures immediately, on a small screen at the back, so you can discard them there and then if the shot is not perfect. Although the initial outlay can be expensive, you will no longer need to buy film or pay for processing because you will be able to do it all yourself using your computer.

## Scanner

These are used to copy items such as photographs or pictures from books and magazines. Whether you have a digital camera or not, these are useful for scanning old photographs into the computer for manipulation or enhancement. This is the key to a lot of the fun – now you can mix your photos with those from a magazine with terrific results. Show your friends a photo of yourself mixing with the rich and famous perhaps! Who said the camera never lies?

## Printer

This is an obvious necessity in order to print out your finished results. Colour photo quality printers can now be purchased at very reasonable prices and there is an abundance of special coated papers available to achieve professional looking results.

## Photo editing program

You will need this piece of software to load your photographs into prior to working on them. With these programs you can adjust colours, take out unwanted parts of the photograph, merge two or three photographs together and much, much more. You will often find that you will get such a program provided with your scanner, although in the main these are quite basic. Keep an eye open for demo versions on the front of magazines – this way you can try before you buy. In this section we have used a program called **Paint Shop Pro**, which is often on magazine cover disks and will enable excellent results to be obtained quite easily.

Fig. 21. The Paint Shop Pro Window.

Figure 21 shows the window of the Paint Shop Pro program with a photograph of a flower that has been scanned in. The icons of the toolbar at the top allow you to quickly turn the palette boxes on and off. These palettes allow control over what you are working with at the time. For example, when you select the paint brushes from the tool palette, the control box palette will allow you to change the size and shape of the brush along with its density and opaqueness, while at the same time the colour palette will allow you to change the colour that the brush will paint.

## GETTING A PHOTOGRAPH INTO THE COMPUTER
### Downloading photographs from a digital camera

A digital camera holds its images on a small disk-like chip inside the body. The amount of images this disk holds varies according to the size (in megabytes) of the disk and the quality (resolution) of the image taken. Most cameras come packaged with a cable to connect it to a computer, via one of the serial ports on the rear of the computer. You will need to load the software program onto your computer to enable you to **download** the images. This action takes a few minutes and during this time uses the power from your camera – a mains power adapter is useful here. The software normally allows the choice of transferring either just selected images, or all shots you have taken. The time it takes varies, again depending on the quantity and quality of the images, but on average it would take around five minutes to download twelve high quality pictures.

Alternatively, there are devices such as **ActionTecs Camera Connect**, which acts as an additional mini external drive to your computer. This plugs in via the parallel port, and powers itself via a two-way splitter from the keyboard port. The mini disk, complete with images, is removed from the camera and inserted into the device to enable transfer. They can be worked on from the mini-drive, or copied from the disk onto your hard drive first, in much the same way as you would copy files from a floppy disk.

### Using a scanner to import pictures

If you own a conventional camera, this does not stop you from using your favourite photographs in your computer. Using a scanner is one of the cheapest ways to get your photographs into your computer. There are many choices as to the type and quality available but one which is most suited to photograph scanning is a **flatbed**. They connect to the computer in one of three ways:

- an adapter card fitted inside the computer case
- a USB connector to the USB port at the back of your computer – ensure your computer has one of these before buying this type
- via the parallel port at the back of your computer – your printer then connects into the back of the scanner; this usually means you can only use one or the other at any given time.

Once connected, you load the supplied software drivers onto your computer and begin scanning. Most scanners provide a program that enables you to set a resolution, an exact area to scan and whether it should be in colour or grey mode. There may be other options to control brightness and contrast as well as other colour controls.

**Performing a scan**

Figure 22 shows the Black Widow scanner program. A page from a holiday brochure has been put under the scanner's lid and the Preview button clicked, which performs a quick pre-scan to enable you to see the image. The correct width and height for the scan can be entered in manually or by resizing the box with the use of the mouse and the cursor as shown – the measurements are then entered automatically so that just the picture of the elephants is scanned.

Fig. 22. The window of a typical scanner program.

The **resolution** is set to 100 dots per inch and we are ready to click Scan. After a bit of whirring, the scanner completes its task and brings up a dialogue box, prompting you to name and save your new image. Hey presto, the job is done. Images that have been scanned in, rather than copied from a digital camera, may be of reduced quality, although this will usually be more evident in photographs which have been enlarged prior to printing.

## Graphic file types

There are many different **formats** in which to save a graphic file and they vary too much to go into any detail in this book. The most popular formats that the majority of editing packages can read and understand are as follows:

1. **BMP – bitmap**. Used by many Windows graphics programs including Paint. If you save an image with the .bmp extension, the file can be placed in the Windows folder and used as a wallpaper on your desktop.

2. **TIF – tagged image format**. A format that is used by many page-layout programs but is not accepted in some drawing packages.

3. **JPEG – joint photographic experts group**. Commonly used for scanned photographs and to output scanned images to the web. This format can display millions of colours but reduces file size dramatically by compressing image data. Many digital cameras save their images to disk in this format.

4. **GIF – graphic interchange format**. Used when colour transition is not important. Only 256 colours or less can be displayed resulting in small file sizes. Used frequently in web page creations.

## Deciding what resolution to use

Scanning resolution is described in dots per inch (dpi), or it may be in pixels per inch. The higher the dpi, the more information the image file contains – therefore the larger the file size becomes. Theoretically, the more information that the file contains, the sharper the image should be. However, there is a limit.

Scanning at a low resolution may produce blurry images, or you may see jagged edges within the image as seen in Figure 23a, which was scanned at 100 dpi. Figure 23b was scanned at 400 dpi and it is noticeable that the image is clearer, but scanning at too high a resolution may equally spoil the image by making it appear flat and lifeless. File size at

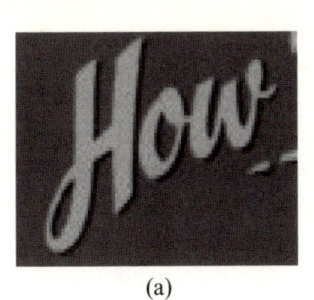

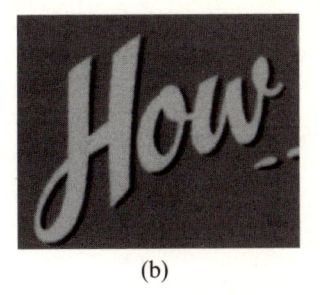

Fig. 23. Showing the difference in dpi resolution.

the scanning stage is also a large consideration in relation to how much RAM memory your computer has. For general purposes a resolution of 300 dpi should be more than sufficient.

## Examples of file sizes at scanning stage and after saving

When scanning a 6 in. × 4 in. colour photograph the file sizes in Table 1 would be typical. The BMP figure would be the size the image is when first scanned. The JPEG figure is the amount of space the file would take up on your hard drive after the file has been converted and saved in this format – quite a difference in file size. But bear in mind that, when working with a file, you are working with its full BMP equivalent size. If you have less than the suggested amount of RAM memory in your computer to work with an image scanned at this resolution, working with the file would be a very hard and slow process for the machine and will need some patience from the user.

Table 1. Examples of file sizes

| Resolution | BMP size | JPEG size | RAM required |
|---|---|---|---|
| 100 | 673KB | 62KB | 4 Meg |
| 200 | 2,687KB | 180KB | 12 Meg |
| 300 | 6,049KB | 380KB | 24 Meg |
| 400 | 10,747KB | 592KB | 48 Meg |
| 600 | 24,179KB | 1,028KB | 96 Meg |
| 1000 | 67,163KB | 2,386KB | 256 Meg |

If you wish to keep your photograph or image around the same measurements as the originals, scanning at 100 or 200 dpi will be sufficient. If you will be enlarging the image, go for 300 or 400 to keep the depth of detail. Above this, you are in the professional league and will need professional equipment to produce the results.

## MANIPULATION TECHNIQUES AND THEIR USES

Once your photo file is on the computer, there will be many options available to you. All of these will require some sort of extra software to enable manipulation. You can get programs that will position all of your photographs in the computer's equivalent of a photograph album on the screen. You may put your pictures into categories such as Weddings, Holidays, etc. for them to be viewed in the same grouping.

If you wish to do a little more to your photos than just display them you will need other software such as an **image editing package** – Paint Shop Pro and Adobe PhotoShop are two examples. With these types of program, you open your file and the sky is the limit. You can carry out relatively simple operations from lightening or sharpening an image to adding all sorts of weird and wonderful filters such as hot wax coatings and canvas appearance. An item or area of one photograph can be drawn around carefully with the Lasso tool – enabling you then to cut out that part of the photo and paste it into another one.

Figure 24 shows how, first, the adult elephant is cut out and placed onto the photograph with the hills and water background, followed by the baby elephant using the same method. The last photo, which gives the effect that the elephants are walking on water, is saved under a separate name for display on a web page.

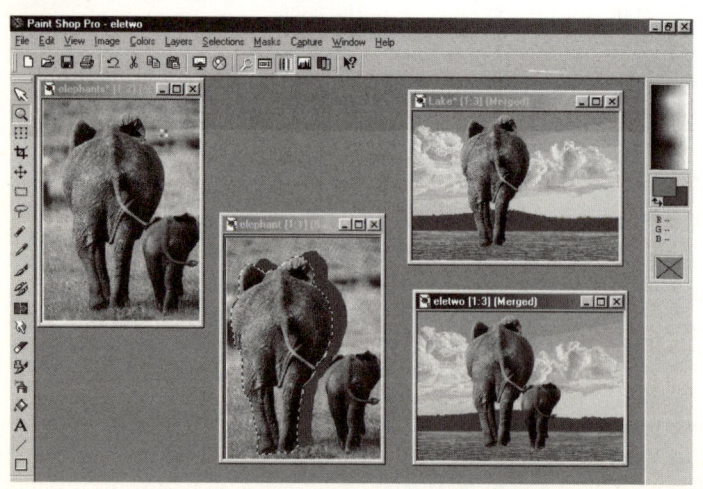

Fig. 24. Clever tricks with manipulation.

## Two things to remember before we begin

1. Working with photographs can be very rewarding but a lot of time and effort needs to be applied. It is because of this that you are strongly recommended to **save your work often**. Always save a copy of your originals in a separate directory, this way you can always be sure that they are preserved and you will be able to compare finished results with originals.

2. Your biggest friend is the **Undo** command found in the Edit menu. Each time you do something to your photo it is recorded in the undo history. This allows you to undo all previous actions. It is useful for trying various changes – apply a filter, if you don't like it, **Undo** it and try another. But beware that once you save an image or close down the program, the undo history clears!

## Putting the manipulation tools to use

We will now have a closer look at some of the tools you will use to edit your photographs. We are using Paint Shop Pro 5.0 because it is easily available and can perform most of the functions we will need. The tools indicated in Figure 25 will also be available in many other packages. Although the icons may be slightly different, the actual tools will work in much the same way.

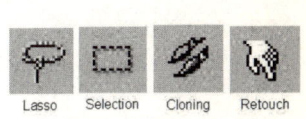

Fig. 25. Manipulation tool icons.

## Cutting around odd shapes with the Lasso

This tool was used to cut the selection of the elephants for our earlier example. It requires a bit of practice to use and quite a bit of care. A steady hand is a definite advantage. Once the tool has been selected the cursor changes to a lasso with a crosshair. The crosshair is like a gun sight and is used to guide the lasso around the object you are selecting. This is used to select an object with an irregular outline and enables you to draw freehand around it.

- First, select the icon and position the crosshair where you wish to start the outline.
- Click and hold down the left mouse button and carefully guide the crosshair to trace around the object.
- Keep your finger on the mouse button until you have finished tracing or you may have to start the procedure all over again.

- It is not necessary to join the start and finish points together, that will be done for you when you release the mouse button.

- When you have completed your trace the border will be seen as a dashed line.

### Making life easier with Smart Edge
Now you have tried it the hard way, have a go the easy way. With the Lasso tool selected, toggle the control palette on. From the Tool Controls tab select **Smart Edge** as shown in Figure 26. Now, when you draw round the shape, instead of holding the mouse button down, just click it at small space intervals. Smart edge will attempt to trace the contour of each edge in between your clicks until you join the starting and finishing points together.

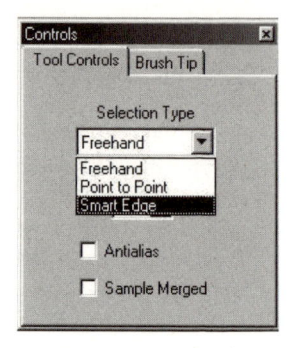

Fig. 26. Changing selections with control palette.

### Then the fun begins
The area within the border is now treated as the selection you are working with and can be handled in a number of different ways. It can be cut or copied, flipped, a filter applied to it, lightened, darkened, etc. Most of the commands you require will be found in the Edit or Image menus at the top of the page or as tools on the toolbar. If you wish to remove the selection, then choose cut. If you are going to use the selection in another photo, then choose copy as this will keep the original image intact.

### Picking out areas with the Selection box
Sorry, no chocolates in this one! If you wish to select an area of a particular shape, then use the rectangular **Selection** tool. Once this tool is selected, you can then toggle the control palette on to change the shape of the selection you wish to make.

- If you select a rectangle or square, position the crosshair at the top left corner of where your selection is to begin.

- With a circle or ellipse, the crosshair should be placed in the centre of your selection.

- Click and hold down the left mouse button while dragging the cross-

hair to the diagonally opposite corner or outwards for a round selection.
- Let go of the mouse button to see your selected area.
- This selection is then defined as the working area, as with the Lasso.

**Copying with the Cloning tool**

Bags of fun to be had with this one. The Cloning tool, also known as the **rubber stamp** in some packages, is probably one of the most useful tools for touching up photographs you will ever come across. It should be used in conjunction with the **brush control box** that we will look at shortly.

Once selected, the cursor will change to a picture of a paint brush with a rubber stamp alongside it. The tool clones/copies a target area of the image to another place.

- First you place the cursor on an area of the image you wish to copy then click and release the **right** mouse button. Nothing appears to have happened at this point but don't worry.
- Next move the cursor to the position on the image that you want your copy to appear.
- Now click the left mouse button and hold it down. You will notice that a cross has appeared at the point on the image that you right-clicked.
- If you continue to hold down the left button and slowly move the mouse around you will see two things happening. Firstly, the cursor and the cross both move in exactly the same way. Secondly, whatever the cross moves over, that image will appear at the cursor.

Figure 27 shows how the cloning tool can copy a foot. This appears really spooky at first but as you experiment you will begin to realise just how powerful this tool really is. Instead of moving the mouse around with the button held down, try just clicking and releasing – this will demonstrate why it is sometimes referred to as the rubber stamp. It is also possible to clone from one image to another providing they are of the same type, i.e. both images are grey scale or both

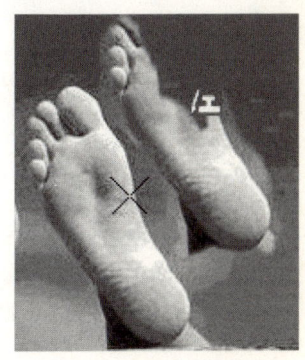

Fig. 27. The wonders of cloning.

images are 256 colours. This gives you unbelievable power over your photographs.

## Putting the cloning tool to good use

This tool is particularly useful for removing those annoying things that spoil a good photo. You have probably had your holiday photos come back from the developers with a beautiful view ruined by the huge red crane that you could have sworn wasn't there when you took it. No problem.

1. Scan the photo into Paint Shop Pro.
2. Zoom in so that you can work more accurately.
3. Select the clone tool.
4. Drop the cross on the area immediately next to the crane.
5. Position the cursor on the crane and hold down the left mouse button.
6. Gently move the cursor around and the crane disappears.

As you can see with Figure 28, the Cloning tool can be very effective and it is well worth the time spent getting the hang of it. When using colour photographs, the effects are even more remarkable.

Fig. 28. Removing an eyesore.

## Tidying up with the Retouch tool

The Retouch tool is again used very much in conjunction with the **control palette**, which we will look at next. This allows you to make the final adjustments to your photo editing. On occasions, in fact on most occasions, when you have cut a selection and pasted it onto another

# Fulfilment with Photograph Editing 45

area of the picture, there will be a sharp line around the outside. This occurs because of slight inaccuracies in the original selection or sharply contrasting background colours. After merging the two layers, the retouch tool on the *smudge* or *soften* setting gently blends the outlines into each other eliminating this sharpness entirely.

## Setting requirements with the control palette

The control palette has two tags – **Tool Controls** and **Brush Tip**. Each tab allows different settings to be chosen, depending on which tool is selected. We saw earlier how the tool control tab was used with the Lasso tool to change it to Smart Edge, but with the Retouch tool it has options such as **soften** and **smudge**. The Brush Tip tab as shown in Figure 29 has various options available for setting the physical design of the brush.

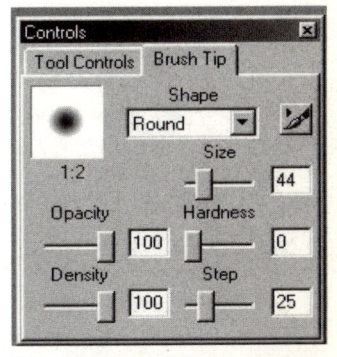

Fig. 29. Setting the brush sizes.

As you alter the characteristics, the small window on the left reflects them. You will have to experiment with different shapes and sizes to find the correct one for the job you are doing. In general the higher the magnification of the image, the smaller the brush you will need. The smallest brush is one pixel or dot and the largest will cover an area 200 pixels square. Hardness is normally set at zero to give a smoother edge so that alterations don't stand out like a sore thumb.

## SOME OTHER IDEAS OF PRACTICAL USES

### Colour adjustment

Sometimes a photo that looks as if it will never be suitable for the family album can be rescued using the commands listed under this menu. If it is too dark then it can be lightened and you will be surprised at how much this can improve its appearance. This is the first option under the **Colour** menu. Also in this selection is the ability to adjust the colour mix. Sometimes, a photo taken with flash can give a person a sickly greenish tinge. To cure this, just try adding a little more red – the difference is amazing.

### That old-fashioned look
Colour photographs can be given an old-fashioned look by converting them into black and white or by going one step further and giving them the sepia look. Both these effects can be achieved in the Colour menu. Choose **grey scale** to convert to black and white or colourise to adjust the hue and saturation for sepia. If you are using a black and white original you may need to click on '**increase colour depth**' before the colourise option is available. Set hue and saturation to 45 as a starting point.

### Removing red-eye or re-colouring eyes
Photographs that show people with red eyes where the flash has caught them can be adjusted in image-editing software. Zoom in close on the eyes and select the red pixels with either the magic wand or one of the selection tools. From the **Colour** menu select **Adjust** then **Hue/Saturation/Luminance.** In the dialogue box reduce the saturation to minus figures – this removes the red without obscuring existing detail. The same pixels can then be given a colour using the colourise option from the same menu. Change the hue and saturation values till you reach the colour you require.

### Removing scratches from photos
By zooming in to a scratched area and careful use of the Cloning tool, scratches or creases can be removed from crumpled photos.

We hope that this chapter has given you some ideas for practical purposes and a bit of fun. Photo editing can take time and patience but the rewards are very gratifying.

### CASE STUDY

### Jenna gives her great-grandmother a facelift
Jenna has been tracing her family tree and has been scanning into her computer any photographs of relatives that she can obtain from her family. Her mother produces a very old photograph of Jenna's great-grandmother. It is the only photograph still around of her, so she is told to be careful with it, as it is already badly creased and scratched.

Jenna takes the photograph home and scans it into her computer at a resolution of 300 dpi. Using Paint Shop Pro she very carefully removes the blemishes and creases with the Clone and Smudge tools. The whole operation takes Jenna just one evening. When she has finished, she prints two enlarged copies for her mother and grandmother as Christmas gifts.

## PRACTICAL EXERCISE

For this exercise, you will need a copy of Paint Shop Pro. The latest version can usually be found and downloaded from www.shareware.com. The only other thing you need is a picture, drawing or photograph. We have used a drawing called Car. This was found in the C:\Program Files\Microsoft Office\Clipart\Popular folder. If you have Microsoft Office on your computer, check out this folder for the same drawing.

1. Start Paint Shop Pro and open a drawing by clicking on **File\Open** and selecting the file from its location.

2. So that the original file is preserved, select **Save As..** from the **File** menu to save this drawing under a different name.

3. With the copy of your drawing selected, click on the Image menu and select **Deformations**. You will see a list of effects you can apply to your drawing.

4. Choose one of the effects by clicking on the name and watch your drawing change instantly. If you do not like the effect, select **Undo** from the **Edit** menu and try another.

Our samples in Figure 30 were saved as Car1 to Car4. We opened a copy of each and applied a different effect.

- Car1 is a copy of the original drawing to show what it did look like.
- Car2 was given the Perspective – Horizontal deformation.
- Car3 was given the Wind deformation.
- Car4 used the first deformation – the Circle.

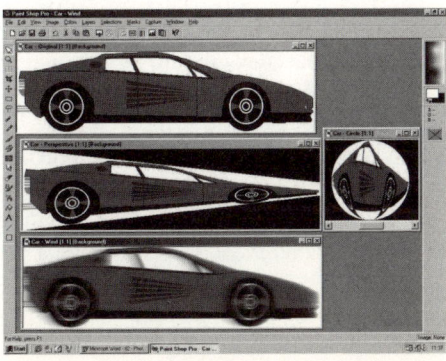

Fig. 30. Various filters applied to a drawing.

# 3

# Making a Word Processor Work More Effectively

If you have had your computer for a while, you will no doubt have experimented with basic formatting such as bold, underline, italics, changing font sizes and aligning text left, right or centre. These are all relatively quick and easy to work with.

We will now look at other types of formatting that are often needed, not necessarily just to improve the look of the document, but to present information in a way that is easier to read and understand.

Later on in the chapter, we will discuss additional programs that can be purchased to enhance the use of your word processor – even if you are unable to get to grips with typing.

## CONSTRUCTING THE LAYOUT WITH COLUMNS AND TABLES

Information in columns can be easier to read because they contain shorter lines. Imagine how difficult a newspaper would be to read with no columns. Most word processors allow their use, but there are two factors to bear in mind:

- A block of ordinary text, such as a story or an article that is split into columns with the need to be read from top left to bottom right, is ideally suited to the use of columns.

- Text that provides snippets of information, such as three separate names and addresses that may contain an unequal amount of lines in each column, would be easier to format with the use of a table.

The reason for this is that in column format, the text flows down one column then continues to the next, filling each line as normal. With the second example, the required line spacing may need to be different in each column as shown in Figure 31. Column format would not allow

## Making a Word Processor Work More Effectively 49

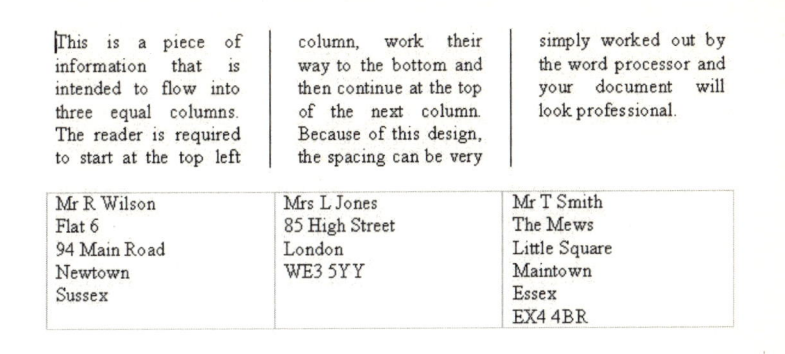

| This is a piece of information that is intended to flow into three equal columns. The reader is required to start at the top left | column, work their way to the bottom and then continue at the top of the next column. Because of this design, the spacing can be very | simply worked out by the word processor and your document will look professional. |
|---|---|---|
| Mr R Wilson<br>Flat 6<br>94 Main Road<br>Newtown<br>Sussex | Mrs L Jones<br>85 High Street<br>London<br>WE3 5YY | Mr T Smith<br>The Mews<br>Little Square<br>Maintown<br>Essex<br>EX4 4BR |

Fig. 31. Different column layouts.

for this and would not space it evenly, therefore altering its appearance.

### The way that columns work

Our example here is worked using Microsoft Word. This program allows you not only to format the whole document to columns, but also to format individual sections of your work. Some other smaller word processors such as Microsoft Works do not allow you to format sections – only the whole document. When this is the case it can be overcome by using the **insert table** format command instead.

Normally the text you type will start at the left side of the page and continue until it reaches the right margin when it will start a new line – this is single column mode. To split the text into more than one column, click on the column command and tell the program how many columns you require. A **section break** is inserted at the point where your cursor is positioned. If you have already started entering text, then this break will be placed at the beginning of the paragraph in which your cursor resides. From this point onwards your text will be flowed into the number of columns you requested until you revert back to normal.

When you go back to normal text, which you do by telling it to format to one column, another section break will be inserted. Any text between these section breaks will be printed in the required number of columns, but anything before the first break or after the last one will show as normal one-column text.

The catch here is that depending on your selected viewing mode, you may not always see a section break, or the columns. As this can leave you feeling a little worried as to whether your printed work will appear as intended, we will look at some tips to make sure you get it right first time.

## Creating text columns

If you work in **Page Layout** mode as selected from the View menu, your work will be **WYSIWYG** (what you see is what you get).

- If you wish to format just a small section, type out your text first and then convert it.
- Ensure that the required text is selected before converting it.
- If your cursor is positioned in the middle of a paragraph, it will change to columns from the beginning of that paragraph onwards until you tell it otherwise.
- If you highlight a particular paragraph, formatting will only apply to that paragraph – unless your word processor will not allow this.
- If you wish to work on each column individually, use the Table feature instead.
- If your program will not create columns for sections of a document, the Table feature can be used to overcome this.

The quickest way to place columns in your document is to ensure that your cursor is at the correct point, or that the required text is selected, then click on the column icon from the toolbar as shown in Figure 32a. Drag your cursor over the number of columns you require and click to select.

If you have more specific requirements, select **format** from the menu titles and choose **columns**. The dialogue box such as the one shown in Figure 32b will allow you to enter the number of columns you require along with other options such as inserting a line in between the columns and whether you wish them to be of equal width.

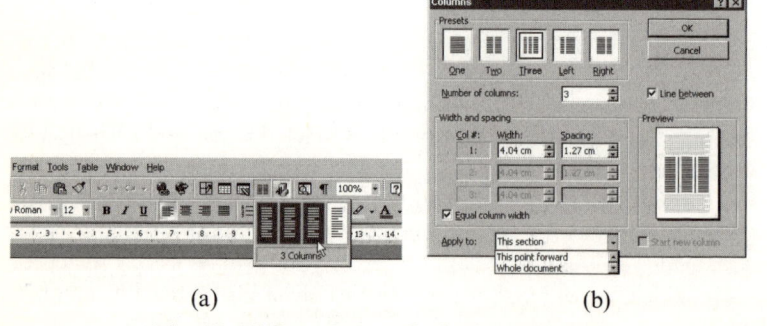

(a)                                    (b)

Fig. 32. Different ways of selecting columns.

## Inserting a table

If your word processor will not allow small sections of text within your document to be formatted as columns, or if you require the information contained in the column to be set out in a particular way, you should use the Table command instead.

Select the icon from the toolbar that represents inserting a table and choose how many columns you wish the table to have by dragging your cursor over the grid. If your table is purely to be used as text columns, you will only need one row as shown in Figure 33. As you type, the cell that is holding the text will expand downwards automatically – you do not need to type each row of text into a different row of the table.

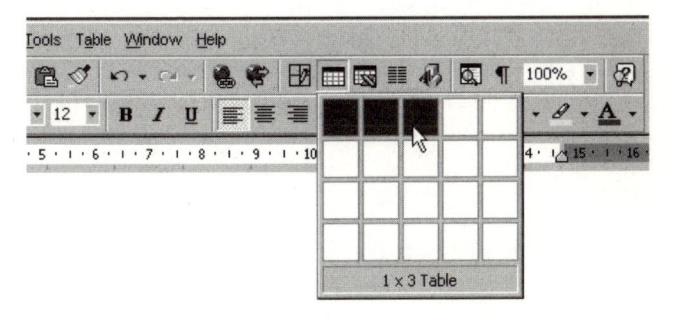

Fig. 33. Inserting a table from the toolbar.

## Getting rid of the borders

Figure 34 shows how a mixture of single and multiple columns can be used within the same document by the insertion of a table. You can see that at present it has a border indicating that it is in fact a table. These borders can be either hidden, or set to **no border** so that your work resembles column text.

|  |  |  |
| --- | --- | --- |
| Your inserted table will look similar to the above box when it is first inserted. | However, when you begin typing text into the first cell of the grid – it will automatically grow. | When you wish to go to the next cell for the next column, use the tab key to move along. |

When you have finished entering your text, click outside the box with your mouse to begin ordinary one column text again.

Fig. 34. Showing multiple and a single column.

To change the border, first select the table, then choose the **Borders** command, usually found on the **Format** menu. The dialogue box will have an option to allow you to set the border to none. Your document may still look as though there are borders there, although greyed out, but if you check out the print preview you will see that they have gone.

### Manipulating the columns

Tables do not have side margins, so occasionally they may make text look too close together. It may not be clear whether you should read across the page or in columns. This can be overcome by inserting extra columns that sit between the ones containing your text. The extra ones are left blank – they are there just to create a feeling of space as shown in Figure 35.

To do this, select a column in your table to the right of where you wish the blank column to appear. From the table menu select **insert column**. You will then have to adjust the width of the new column so that it gives the desired effect.

| The text in this column is very close to the right | It may be unclear whether to read in columns or not | To correct this, insert extra blank columns |
|---|---|---|

The above table has three columns

| The text in this column is very close to the right | | It may be unclear whether to read in columns or not | | To correct this, insert extra blank columns |
|---|---|---|---|---|

This table has five columns, but columns two and four are blank to create space

Fig. 25. Creating space for easy reading.

## CREATING AND PLACING DRAWINGS AND PICTURES

Many word processors now include drawing facilities – this doesn't mean you can get out your crayons and start colouring on your monitor, but it does give you the facility to create illustrations using the given shapes, lines, arrows and text. Different programs may vary in the number of shapes that are provided and the effects that can be achieved with them.

### Creating the drawing

To begin the draw program and access the drawing toolbar, click on the drawing command found on the Insert menu, or you may have an icon on your toolbar. Once selected, you have the option of choosing one of

Making a Word Processor Work More Effectively **53**

the many shapes and placing it within your document. Position the cursor at the point you wish your drawing to begin and drag the cursor to where you wish the shape to finish. You will see it appear as you do so.

There will be options to colour the shape or line from the **colour palette** and you can alter the size in any direction you wish by use of the **handles** around the frame of the shape. Some programs have extra options such as producing shadows and 3D effects. Try experimenting and you will be surprised how quickly an effective illustration can be created.

### Grouping objects together

Often a drawing or graphic will encompass more than one object – it may be a mixture of shapes, lines, graphics and text all rolled into one, as in a logo. To ensure that any formatting applied to the design is done in proportion and to each object, the individual parts need to be grouped together so that it can be treated as one graphic. The command for **grouping** will be found within the toolbar of the drawing program.

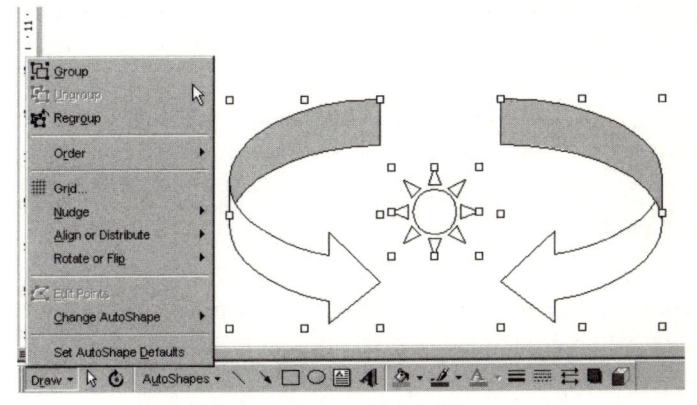

Fig. 36. Grouping multiple objects together.

1. Figure 36 shows three separate objects – two arrows and a star.
2. To group the objects together, they first have to be selected.
3. You select each object in turn while holding down the shift key on your keyboard.
4. Once this is done, click on the **draw** icon, then on **group** for all objects to be locked together.
5. If you now need to move or resize the group, each element will be moved or resized accordingly.

## Inserting graphics

To insert graphics and clipart that has been created elsewhere, first place the cursor where you wish to position the graphic; from the **insert** menu, choose **picture**, then locate the file using the dialogue box provided and click OK.

## Making the objects stay where they are put

It can be a little disconcerting, having placed your graphic just where you want it, to find that, once it appears, the look of your document goes haywire. This is because of the way a word processor handles the graphic. This can be overcome in a number of ways. Once the graphic is in place, use the **format picture** command from within the menu or on the icon toolbar of your program to set your choices of **wrapping** display.

*Working out the wrapping*

Wrapping describes how you want text to behave around an inserted object. There are four main choices, although some word processors will give you more – we will concentrate on the main ones for now as shown in Figure 37.

1. **None** – this means that the text will behave as though there is no graphic there at all, it will go right over the top. This is advantageous when using a pale graphic that you wish to look like a watermark.

2. **Top and Bottom** – this ensures there will be no text either side of the object. Ideal for producing space.

3. **Square or to the frame** – most graphics have a square invisible frame around them that the picture sits inside. The text on this option will read either side of this frame but will not go through it.

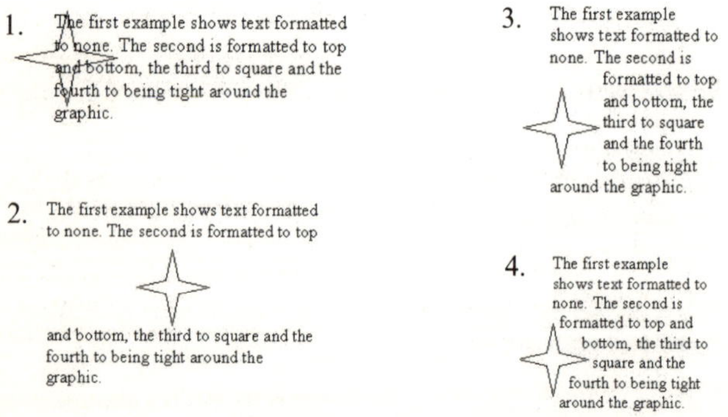

1. The first example shows text formatted to none. The second is formatted to top and bottom, the third to square and the fourth to being tight around the graphic.

2. The first example shows text formatted to none. The second is formatted to top and bottom, the third to square and the fourth to being tight around the graphic.

3. The first example shows text formatted to none. The second is formatted to top and bottom, the third to square and the fourth to being tight around the graphic.

4. The first example shows text formatted to none. The second is formatted to top and bottom, the third to square and the fourth to being tight around the graphic.

Fig. 37. Different wrap settings.

4. **Tight or to the picture** – you may have the option to trim this invisible frame (called **cropping**) so that the text will sit tight up against the actual shape of the graphic. Again it does not go through it.

These will no doubt be described in different ways depending on which word processor you are using, but at least if you know what the intended result is, you will be able to find what you are looking for.

There are two other options that some word processors such as Microsoft Word may have that are worth noting. They are whether your graphic is to **float** with the text or should be **fixed** in its position. If you select the **anchor fixed**, your graphic will stay exactly where you put it – if you do not select this, your graphic will **float** with the text. Floating with the text means that if your text moves from one page to another during editing of a long document, for example, your graphic will move with it. If you have selected **anchor fixed** and you change your document, you may find the graphic is no longer with its relevant text.

## MANIPULATING TABS, BULLETS AND NUMBERING

### Using tabs

Tabs can be very useful for quickly and easily lining up particular pieces of text. In their simplest form, pressing the tab key on your keyboard moves the cursor to the next nearest half an inch. They are used as an easy way of creating columns of text. However, they can also be used for lining up using either left, right, centre or a decimal point alignment of that text as shown in Figure 38.

Along the top of your worksheet you will have something that resembles a ruler – if you cannot see one, check the **View** menu and select **ruler** from the toolbars option. Tabs can be set at the beginning of a new document so they apply all the way through, or they can be set once you get to that part of the document to which you wish them to apply. Individual paragraphs can have different settings by simply changing the tabs as

| Left Aligned | Centre Aligned | Decimal Point | Right Aligned |
|---|---|---|---|
| Julie | Mother | £22.78 | Paid |
| Robert | Father | £9.76 | Paid |
| Sheila | Grandmother | 20p | Unpaid |
| John | Son | £32.00 | Paid |

Fig. 38. Different tab settings.

you get to each one. Any previous settings will remain in effect for that part of the document to which they were applied.

### Setting the required tabs
The way to set the tabs will depend on your word processor, but generally you will need to either double click on the ruler at the spot you wish to insert the tab, or click on the indicator at the left-hand corner of the ruler as seen in Figure 39, in order to select which type of tab you require and then click on the ruler at the spot you wish to place it. Once the tabs are set on the ruler, begin entering your information, when you need to move along to the next tab setting, press the tab key on your keyboard.

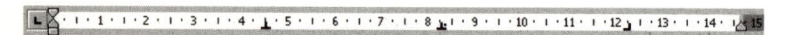

Fig. 39. Tab setting on the ruler.

### Improving the looks of listed information
Information displayed in lists can be made more attractive by use of either bullets or numbers. Numbers are usually used when the information is required to be in a particular order. When there is no importance placed on order, bullets can be used:

- The program will have a selection of different bullets to use...
- and some will have different number displays.
- These are examples from Microsoft Word.
- The list can be created as you go along...
- or you can select a list of text and re-format it...
- with bullets or numbers.

Select **bullets and numbering** from the **format** menu to see the selection that the word processor has to offer, or click the icon on the toolbar to begin a list. With the command selected, each time you press the return key to begin a new line, a bullet or number will automatically precede the following text. To halt the process, either click on the icon again, or you may press the backspace key to remove the last unnecessary bullet.

Numbers can also be displayed in different formats such as the ones below:

| 1) One   | 1. One   | (a) One  | i.   One   |
|----------|----------|----------|------------|
| 2) Two   | 2. Two   | (c) Two  | ii.  Two   |
| 3) Three | 3. Three | (d) Three| iii. Three |
| 4) Four  | 4. Four  | (e) Four | iv.  Four  |
| 5) Five  | 5. Five  | (f) Five | v.   Five  |

**Using the multilevel lists**

Multilevel lists contain two or more levels of bullets or numbering within a single list. Microsoft Word, which we will use to show you an example, allows this to be done with the greatest of ease.

Select the **bullets and numbering** option from the **format** menu and click on the **outline numbered** tab to display the multilevel options available. Select one of the choices then begin creating your list.

1) The text in this example shows as number one, now press the enter key.
2) The number two is automatically put in front of this second line.
   a) To get an indented level like this, press the enter key followed by the tab key
   b) You will continue with a second level indent each time you press the enter key
      i) By pressing enter – followed by the tab again, it will promote the level
      ii) To return to the last level, press enter followed by the tab key but ...
   c) this time hold the shift key down while you press tab.
3) After pressing enter again, and holding down the shift key when pressing tab ...
4) It returns to the first level.

When your list is complete, press the backspace key to clear the last number and stop the listing process. If all this sounds a little difficult to remember, you can convert a list that has already been typed by using the increase indent icon as shown in Figure 40:

Fig. 40. Toolbar icons for various indents.

- Highlight the chosen list
- Select **bullets and numbering** from the **format** menu.
- Choose a format from the **outline numbered** tab.
- Select each line of your list in turn.
- Click the increase indent icon on the toolbar.
- The line will move to the level preceded by the appropriate number.

## EXPLORING VOICE DICTATION, OCR SCANNING AND MACROS

For most of us, typing can be a painfully slow process if you have never been taught the skills necessary to do it correctly. There are two types of program that can be added to your computer to assist the process of typing in information.

### Reading your text in with voice dictation

This is a program that runs alongside your word processor. Two popular programs are **IBM Simply Speaking Gold** and **Voice Power Solo**. Generally, 'the more you pay, the better the benefits' of course. However, even the basic ones can help improve the speed of the two-fingered typist!

The idea is that once they are installed, with the aid of a microphone and speakers, you teach the program to understand your voice and accent. The program will already have a basic vocabulary but will need to learn how you say the words that it can understand. With the guidance of the program, you will need to spend half an hour or so repeating meaningless words or phrases for it to learn. Once taught, you can speak straight into your word processor and see the words appear a lot quicker than you can type them.

### Scanning text with OCR programs

Another useful addition, especially if you regularly re-enter text from a pretyped document, is **Optical Character Recognition (OCR)** programs. These, with the aid of a scanner, photocopy the typed text from the document into the OCR program. At that stage, it is still classed as one complete graphic and cannot be edited. You trim off the parts of the scan that are not relevant, leaving just the text that you wish to import into your word processor. Press the OCR button and the program will go to work converting it from a graphic into text. Once completed it can then be saved into your documents folder and be treated as a normal text document with the usual editing facilities available.

These programs can be a little tricky to set up and should not be relied upon to be 100 per cent accurate, but they can save a lot of time. Once you have got the knack of using them, it will be quicker to correct a few errors than to type a whole document in yourself. Two of the most popular software programs of this type are **Textbridge OCR** and **Omnipage**. Many new scanners will have a basic OCR program packaged with them.

### Speeding up entries with macros

A **macro** is a recording that you create from a sequence of keystrokes all rolled into one. If you find you are repetitively entering the same information, you can record it so that when you press the key you have assigned to the job, it inserts the recorded text for you in a flash. For example, if most times that you open a new document you find yourself typing in your address, telephone number and the date – you can make a recording of this so that all you do in the future is press a particular key and it is done for you.

Macros can be used in many programs, not just word processors. Our example of creating them is done using Microsoft Word, but they can be created in Excel, Access, Word Pro and many others, although they may be called something slightly different such as **scripts**.

We will now create a macro that enters the address, telephone number and date on a document (see Figure 41):

1. From the tools menu select **macro**, then **record new macro**.

2. In the **macro name** box enter a short descriptive name with no spaces.

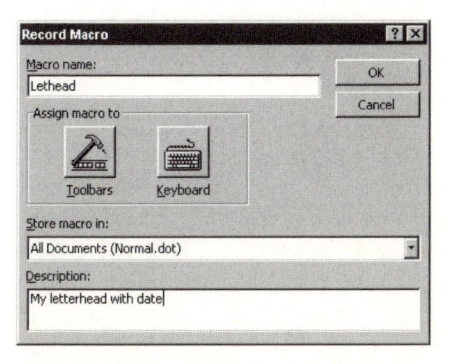

Fig. 41. Getting ready to record a macro.

3. A fuller representation may be entered in the **Description** box.

4. Choose whether you wish to assign a keystroke to your macro...

5. or whether you would like an icon on the toolbar that you can click.

*Selecting the toolbar option*
If you decide on the toolbar option, the dialogue box will then show your macro in the commands box. Select it using your mouse, hold down the mouse button and drag the macro to an empty space on the toolbar – next to the help icon is usually free – then let go of the mouse button. You can now right-click on your new macro button and select a new icon for it using the **change button image** command. Then, in the name box, you can rename it with a more suitable description. When you are finished, click on the close button in the customise dialogue box and you're ready for **recording your macro.**

*Selecting the keyboard option*
If you would rather assign a keystroke, then click on the keyboard option. The dialogue box will require you to enter your preferred keystroke for the macro you are creating. They are usually used in conjunction with the Alt key on your keyboard, so press and hold the Alt key then, for example, the number 1 key. Underneath the keystroke box a description will inform you if that keystroke is already assigned to something else. Providing it isn't, click the **Assign** box, then click on **close** and you are ready for **recording your macro**.

## Recording your macro

You will now see the mouse cursor with a picture of a cassette tape attached, plus a **stop recording** box on your screen as shown in Figure 42 – you are ready to record your macro. Go carefully, because everything that you do now is being recorded, mistakes and all.

6. To start the macro, click on the new document icon on the toolbar.

7. Select your typeface, font size and other requirements for your address such as bold and centralised.

8. Type in your details, then press enter until you are at the line to insert your date.

9. Turn off the bold feature if you want your date in ordinary text.

10. Click on *Insert* from the menus and choose **date and time**.

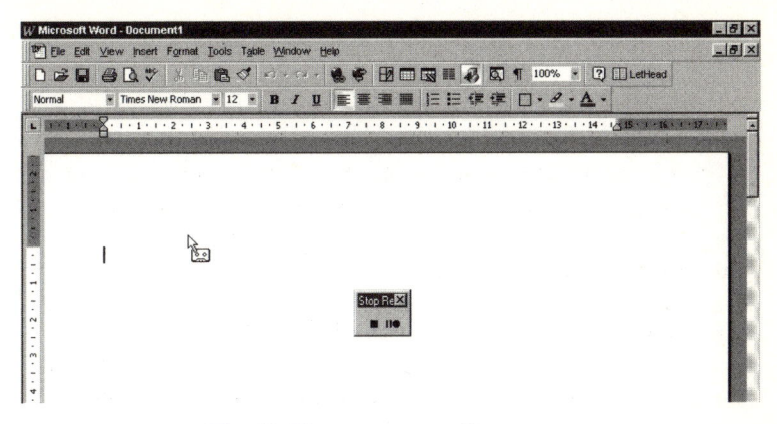

Fig. 42. The macro recording screen.

11. Select the format in which you wish your date to appear and click OK.

12. Now press the enter key again and position your cursor to begin typing your letter.

13. Your macro is complete, so press the square in the **stop recording** button.

You can now close that document – you don't need to save it. To try out your macro, either click the icon that you created on the toolbar, or key in the sequence you assigned, not forgetting the Alt key as well if you used it.

## EXPLAINING FILE CONVERSION FOR IMPORTING/ EXPORTING

There are many occasions when people may wish to write a document on one computer, then save it to a floppy disk in order to use it on a different computer. If both computers have the same word processing program installed, this does not pose any problems but inevitably, with the number of programs available these days, it is quite possible that sooner or later, this will not be the case.

Not all programs save their files in the same way, indeed different versions of the same manufacturer may also save them in slightly different formats. In order for dissimilar programs to understand the same file, they have to be saved in a format that all can understand.

We will use a brief example that deals with text only, if you have charts or graphics within your document it becomes much more complicated and could merit a book all of its own.

Rule number one is always to save your document in the usual way first – this is so your word processor has a copy of the original document the way you intended. Saving to a different format can lose certain layouts that you applied to your document such as bolding and columns, which may have to be reapplied when used in the other program.

**Choosing a format**

Once you are sure you have your copy saved correctly in its original format, with the document still open, click on the **save as** command from the **file** menu. As shown in Figure 43, open the **file type** box and have a look at what other formats you have the option to save in. If you know the version and make of the other program that will be opening your document, and it is listed, then select that. If you are unsure then you need to go for one of the universal formats such as:

- RTF (Rich Text Format)
- ASCII (American Standard Code for Information Interchange)
- Windows Write
- Text.

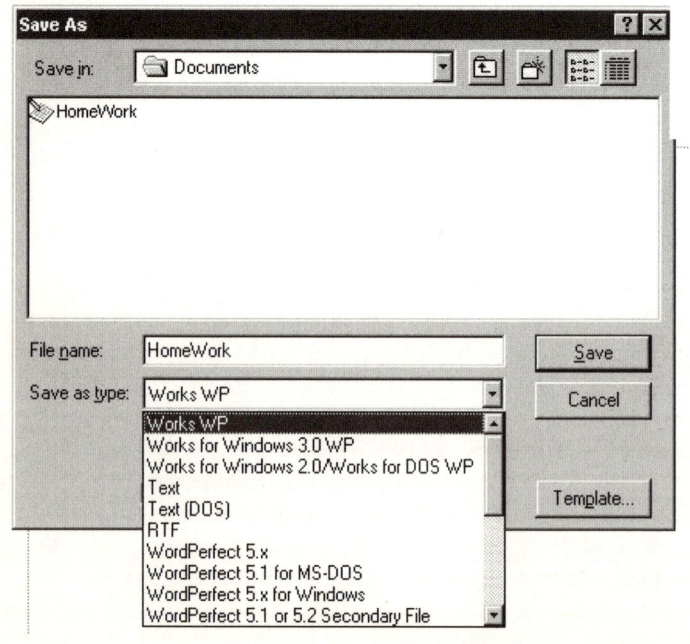

Fig. 43. Saving a file in a particular format.

## Opening the document on the other computer

To open the file you will first need to click on the **file type** box and select the same format as the file was saved in. You should then be able to see your file listed in the dialogue box – you can then select it and open it. Check the layout and correct any conversion errors that may have occurred. Save it once again using the **save as** command, but in the relevant word processor's own format.

## CASE STUDY

### Peter smartens up his neighbourhood-watch.

Peter runs his local neighbourhood-watch committee and has been producing their monthly newsletter for the last six months. Although the committee have been pleased with his efforts, he wants to produce something more professional looking and more attractive to read.

He decides to use a bold heading and to split the main body of the text into three columns. He then designs a simple logo and places it in the centre of the page to get the reader's attention. To finish he flows the columns around the logo to create a border. The end result is a newsletter which looks interesting and which people will be more likely to read and remember.

## PRACTICAL EXERCISE

In this exercise you will save a document in your word processor and open it with Windows own built-in word processor. You will see from saving it in different formats, how word processors can interpret the format instructions in different ways, thereby altering the look of your document.

1. Begin by opening a new document in your word processor.
2. Type in your name and address using one of the less popular fonts such as Script and centre it on the page.
3. Now revert to left alignment and insert today's date using the **insert date** command from the menu titles.
4. Move down the page a little and type in a few lines of text using a common font such as Times New Roman. Insert a few bullets if you like as shown in Figure 44.
5. Save your document in the usual way – to a floppy disk if you wish – naming it **Test1**.

**64** Moving On from Computer Basics

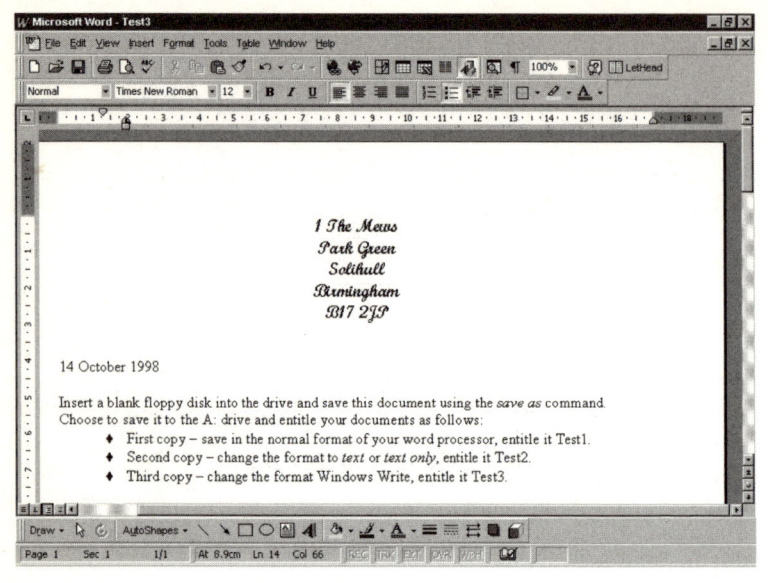

Fig. 44. Some sample text.

6. Now click the **save as** command – you are going to save your document again, but first change the type of format that you are saving it as, to **text** or **text only**, and rename your document **Test2**

7. Repeat the above step, but this time using the Windows Write format and calling it **Test3**.

8. If you do not have the Windows Write format available in the file type box, use the **Rich Text Format (.rtf)** instead. When saving the same documents in different formats it is not essential to change the name of the file – we are just doing this for ease of differentiating between the file types when reopening them.

9. Close down your word processor and open the Windows Wordpad – you will find it in the **Programs**, **Accessories** menu near the bottom. In Windows 3.1x it is called Windows Write.

10. Click on the open command, select the floppy disk drive on the **Look in** box and change the **file types** setting to *.* or **all documents** as shown in Figure 45. You will now see all three of your files. If you look closely, you will see that each icon for the three separate files is different –this denotes the different file type that each document is saved as.

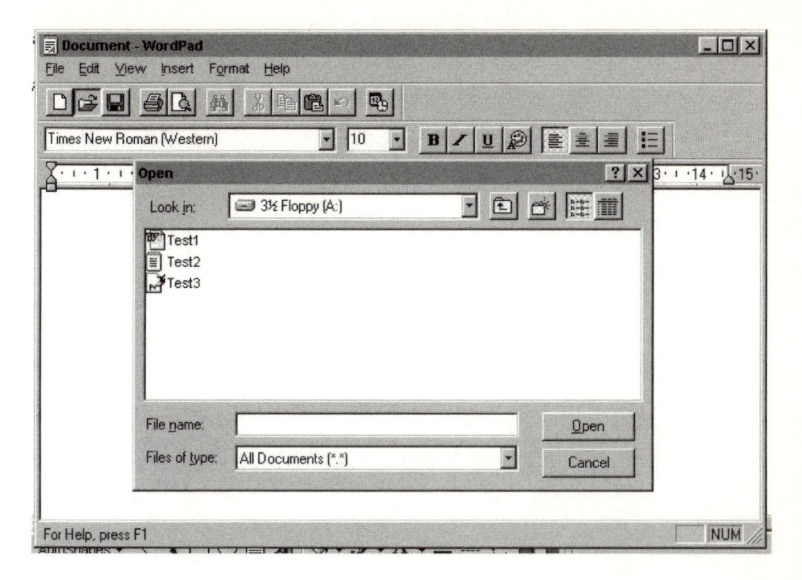

Fig. 45. Have you saved the three files correctly?

11. Change the **file type** box settings to show only those files with **text documents (.txt).** Only Test2 should now be showing – select it and open it.

12. Now do the same again, changing the file type to **Windows Write (.wri)** and opening Test3.

13. Finally, see if your word processor is listed in the file types – if so, choose this and open Test1.

14. If your word processor is not listed, change the file type to all files again, then select Test1 and open it that way.

# 4

# Enhancing the Work of Spreadsheets

A spreadsheet is the ideal program for creating single page forms, charts and tables – these can be anything from a household expense table to a graph that's needed for homework. Don't let this mislead you, however. A spreadsheet can be an extremely powerful mathematical tool comprising thousands of formulae and calculations.

The program's first look is not very appealing. The row of numbers down the side and columns headed with letters making equal-sized little boxes, called cells, can look very boring and unattractive. In this chapter we are going to show you how to make that table or chart look much much better. Our examples are based on **Excel 97** but most packages have similar features.

## MAKING YOUR WORKSHEET MORE ATTRACTIVE

It is assumed you will understand the basics of entering information into a spreadsheet cell, and how simple formulae can perform tasks to save you time and effort. If you do not, we covered this subject in our previous book *Managing Your First Computer*.

### Altering the size of the cell

The column width and row height can be made larger or smaller by the following method. In the grey area of the letters/numbers headings, place the cursor on the line that separates the cell you wish to alter and its adjacent cell. The cursor will change to a double-headed arrow – hold down the mouse button and move the line in the direction required to resize the cell. In Figure 46, column F is being made smaller so that the two charts are closer together.

Adjusting the size of columns can make a table look more attractive straight away. For example, if a table had equal-sized cells but was showing text titles in one column and two digit figures in the next column as in our first chart in Figure 46, either the numbers would look lost in

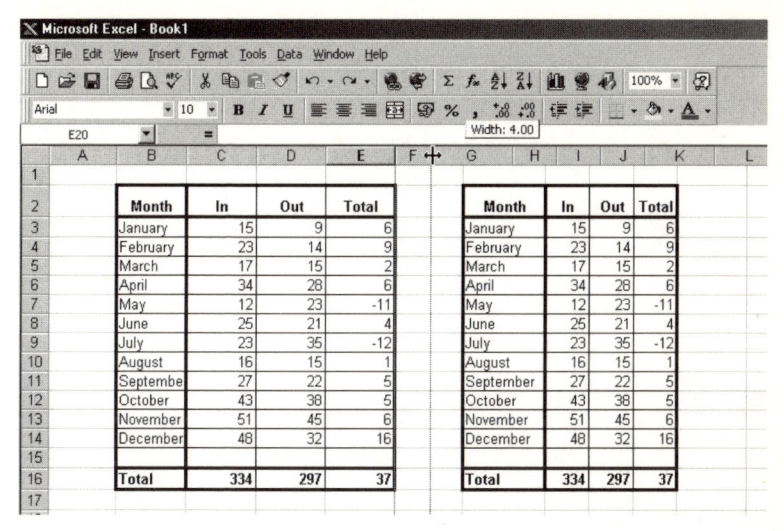

Fig. 46. Altering the width of columns.

large cells or the text would looked cramped and maybe truncated in small cells. The second chart looks much neater with adjusted column widths.

The cells can also be adjusted in other ways giving control over the exact size of the columns/rows.

1. Select the column, row or cell that you wish to resize.
2. From the **format** menu, choose **column** for altering the width, or **row** for changing the height.
3. Here, there are two options:
   (a) **auto** automatically sizes your selection neatly around the text already inserted
   (b) **width/height** allows you to enter the exact size you want your selection to be.

If multiple columns and rows have been selected, they can be adjusted at the same time.

## Positioning the titles

The title headings that explain what information your columns and rows contain sometimes need to be spread over more than one cell. We will show two ways of doing this. One is to merge cells, and the other is to centralise the selection.

**68** Moving On from Computer Basics

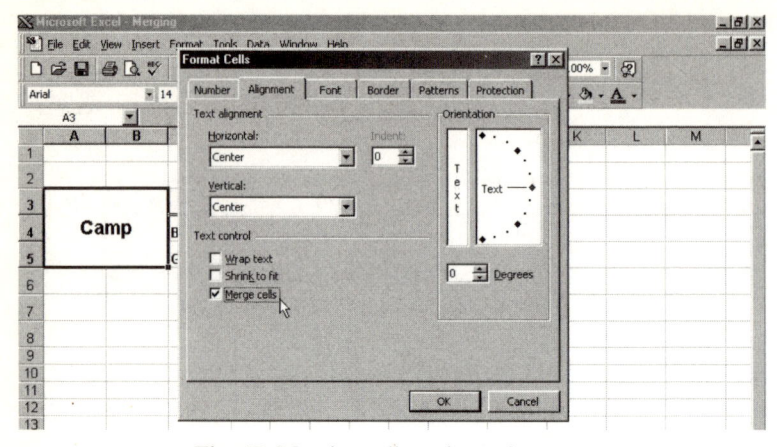

Fig. 47. Merging cells and centring text.

*Merging selected cells*

- Select a group of adjacent cells – A3 to B5 in our example.
- From the **format** menu, choose **cells**.
- Click on the alignment tab.
- Tick the box to **merge cells**.
- Adjust the text alignment in the horizontal/vertical boxes to suit.

The selected cells are now merged as shown in Figure 47 with inserted text 'Camp'. Both the vertical and horizontal alignment was set to **centre** so that the text was neatly positioned in the centre of the merged box.

*Centralising your selection*

- Type in your text – 'Ages of Children' is our example.
- Select the group of adjacent cells that your text needs to cover – D2 to H2.
- From the **format** menu, choose **cells**.
- Click on the alignment tab.
- From the horizontal text alignment box, choose **centre across selection**.

In this example, there is no need to merge the cells.

## Adding borders and lines

Each cell in a spreadsheet has four sides and each can be individually given a border. If a group of cells are selected together, the border can be placed on any of the outside edges, forming a line or a box, and on the inside edges to form a grid. The border types are varied – they can be thick, thin, double-lined, dotted, etc. They can be formatted to a particular colour or indeed a mixture of all.

|   | A | B | C | D | E | F | G | H |
|---|---|---|---|---|---|---|---|---|
| 1 |   |   |   |   |   |   |   |   |
| 2 |   |   |   | Ages of Children ||||
| 3 |   |   |   | 10 | 11 | 12 | 13 | 14 |
| 4 |  Camp || Boys | 3 | 5 | 5 | 4 | 6 |
| 5 |   |   | Girls | 1 | 7 | 2 | 3 | 3 |
| 6 |   |   |   |   |   |   |   |   |

Fig. 48. Adding borders.

In Figure 48, cells C3 to H3 were selected and given a double-lined border just on the bottom edge. Then cells C3 to C5 were selected and given the same double border, but on the right edge. If a chart was showing figures, you might wish to select the total cell and put a double-lined border on the top and bottom edges to enhance it as you would see on accountancy sheets. To achieve these results follow these simple steps:

- Highlight the cells to place a border or line.
- From the **format** menu, choose **cells** and select the **border** tab.
- Figure 49 shows how to make your selections by clicking on the relevant button.

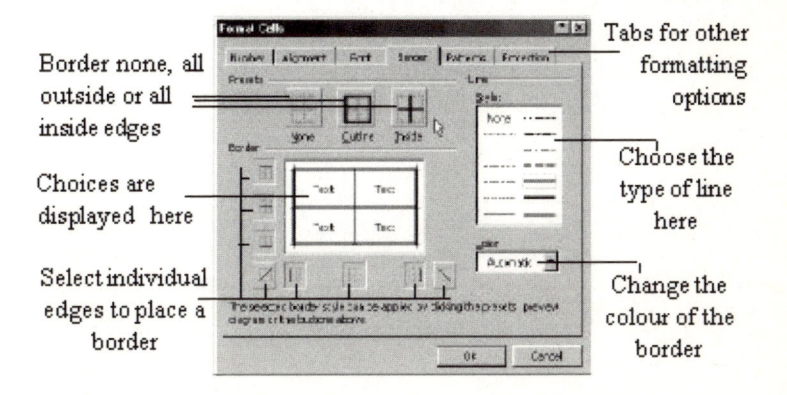

Fig. 49. The border formatting box.

## Entering repetitive information

The **copy** and **paste** commands can be used in a spreadsheet in the same way as in a word processor, although a little care has to be taken when copying formulae to ensure the copied formula takes its information from the correct cells.

When entering information that has a pattern to it, such as days of the week, months of the year, or numbers that increase or decrease in a particular way, the **series** command can be a useful tool.

*How do I quickly fill in a series of numbers or dates?*
The fill series can be used in adjacent horizontal or vertical cells. The first entry has to be typed into the cell – let's say this is January and we wish to fill another eleven cells in the column with the remaining months of the year. Right-click and hold the mouse button on the small square at the bottom right corner of the cell, then drag the cursor over the next eleven empty cells. The cells become highlighted and a menu pops up to select the series you wish to fill, as shown in Figure 50. Click on **fill months** and voila! the cells are filled with February, March, April, etc.

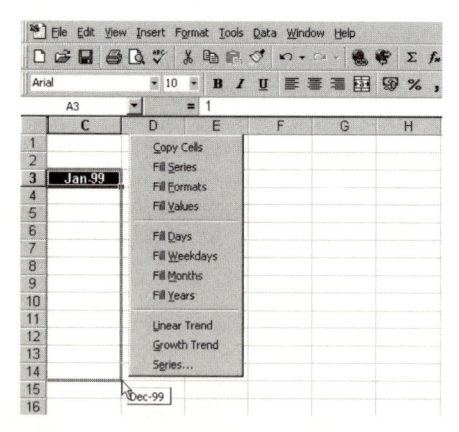

Fig. 50. Using the fill series.

This fill series can be used for regular common increases, such as days of the week, numbers, dates, etc. and also for irregular patterns such as every other day or every other number. In order to do this you must put in the first two entries for the program to find the difference. This is how to do it:

1. Enter the first bit of information – let's say the number 1.

2. In the second cell, enter the next figure in the trend – if we wanted to list all odd numbers, we would enter the number 3.
3. Highlight the two cells. A border appears with a small square in the bottom right corner of the highlighted area.
4. Right-click and hold on the square and drag the cursor, continuing to highlight the area you wish to fill.
5. From the menu choose **linear trend** – this takes the difference between the first and second cells and continues the pattern, i.e. 1, 3, 5, 7 and so on.
6. If you were to choose **growth trend**, it would look at the growth between the two numbers, i.e. multiplying by three, and continue this trend listing 1, 3, 9, 27 and so on.

## Rearranging a list into ascending or descending order

A list of information can be sorted into ascending or descending order at the click of a button. Once your list is entered, highlight all the relevant cells and click on the A–Z icon on the toolbar for ascending order – or the Z–A icon for descending order as shown in Figure 51. This works with text, numbers and dates, but is not so clever with days of the week, or months, as it puts these into alphabetical order instead of chronological order!

Fig. 51. Toolbar icons for information order.

## Adding colour to the worksheet

Plain black lines on a white background can be very hard on the eyes. Adding a little colour can make your work look more interesting, appealing and easier to understand.

- Highlight the cells to be coloured.
- From the **format** menu choose **cells**.
- Click on the **patterns** tab.
- Click on the colour of your choice.
- Click OK.

## What if I don't have enough imagination?

Then you could use the **autoformat**. Enter all your information, highlight and from the **format** menu click on **autoformat**. This option allows you to spruce up your work with colour, borders and text styles in one swoop by selecting one of the pre-prepared styles as seen in Figure 52. Each style can be viewed first showing an example.

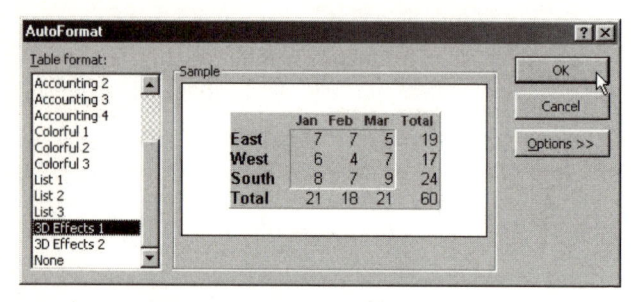

Fig. 52. The autoformat dialogue box.

## CREATING A CHART FROM A TABLE

Excel makes it very easy to convert information into a chart with the **chart wizard**. This can be found on the toolbar and resembles a three-block column chart. The information to be used has to be highlighted before clicking on the wizard. Titles to describe the $x$ and $y$ axes information can be added afterwards as can a main title for the chart.

From our example, we selected the group of information covering the children's ages and sex, which was cells C3 to H5, and then clicked on the wizard icon.

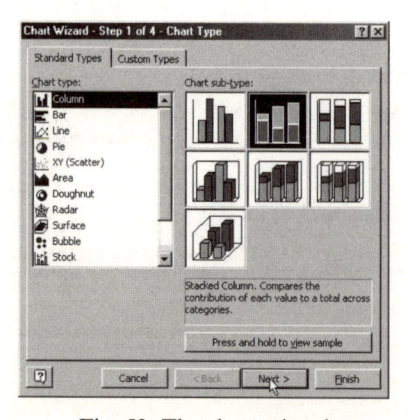

Fig. 53. The chart wizard.

As seen in Figure 53, a choice box is displayed showing the range of charts available from bar and column types to doughnuts and radar! There is also an opportunity to choose between showing the chart in 3D or normal flat mode plus whether to show the actual figures or a conversion of the figures into percentages. As each example is clicked on, a description of what will be shown is displayed underneath.

Once the choices have been made from the types box, clicking on the **next** button allows the choice between showing the information from the rows or the columns. Clicking on **next** again provides boxes to enter the chart title and descriptions for $x$ and $y$ axes. Finally, you have the option to display the chart on the same worksheet as the table, or in a separate worksheet. Click **finish** to complete the chart.

## Making the chart look more interesting

By right-clicking on any individual part of the chart, you can format it to your liking. For example, you could add colour to the **walls**, as they are called. The wall is the background area behind the blocks. The colours of the blocks can be altered, the titles can be formatted to have shadows – you can even make the whole background of the chart display your favourite photograph by selecting the **fill effects** option and choosing the **picture** tab. The design possibilities are limited only by your own imagination.

The chart as a whole can be resized by clicking near the edge to select the chart and then using the sizing handles around the outside in the usual way. The larger the chart is displayed, the more information that may be shown. If the chart is shrunk, some of the figures on the axis may be represented by small dashes on the axis line, but the descriptions will only show every other one. This will be particularly true if the chart is very complex. An example of our finished chart can be seen in Figure 54.

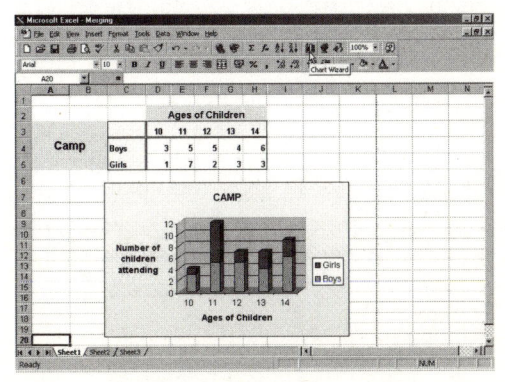

Fig. 54. A finished table and chart.

## SETTING THE PRINT REQUIREMENTS

Printing a spreadsheet has a few differences compared to, say, a word processor. You still have the option to print just certain pages and a specified number of them, etc., but there are extra options of printing specific parts of a worksheet, and choosing whether the gridlines are to be printed or not.

### Printing of charts

A chart that is incorporated into a worksheet will be printed along with the table as part of the file. However, they can be printed independently of each other using the following method:

1. Select the chart by clicking on it, then go to **print preview** mode. Your chart will be displayed filling the whole page: click on **print** if this is correct.

2. Alternatively, click on the **setup** option. On the **page** tab you can change the orientation of the page, but the chart will still fill the whole area.

3. By clicking on the **chart** tab, you can alter the size of your chart. Choosing the **custom** option will resize your chart to its true measurements.

### Printing the table independently of the chart

As stated earlier, the default setting, if the chart is not selected, is to print the table and chart together as a whole file. If you wish to print just the table, or even only part of a worksheet, a print area has to be set first.

1. Highlight the part that needs to be printed by clicking on the top left cell and dragging the cursor to the bottom right cell of the area.

2. From the **file** menu, select **print area**, and then **set print area** as seen in Figure 55. On your worksheet, a faint dotted line will appear around the area that you have set to print.

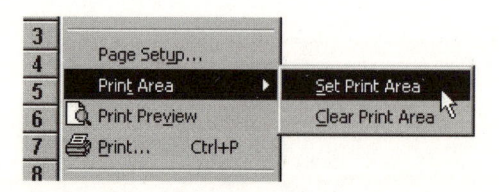

Fig. 55. The print area options.

3. This can be checked by looking in **print preview** mode. Print as normal.
4. If the area is incorrect, or needs changing, select **clear print area** from the **file** menu and repeat the procedure. A print area must be cleared before it can be reset.

## Printing the gridlines

Some spreadsheet packages do not automatically print the gridlines as you see them on the screen – Excel is one of these. However, you can change this:

- From the **file** menu, select **page setup**.
- Click on the **sheet** tab
- Tick the **gridlines** box from the **print** section half-way down.

This will only print the gridlines in between the areas where information is written. If you need gridlines printed in areas where there is no information, set the print area as described above.

Hopefully you will have now gained enough knowledge to create an attractive table or chart and be able to print them out for all to see.


## AN INTRODUCTION TO USING CONTROLS

In this last section we are going to take you through a practical exercise of creating an impressive-looking form that will introduce you to the capabilities of Excel and other spreadsheet programs. You will be able to use most of the formatting techniques already covered in this chapter but learn quite a bit more too. It is quite a time-consuming exercise that will need a fair bit of concentration. You may not understand some of the reasons for doing certain operations, but if the end result gives you a taster for wanting to learn more, there are many good books that cover the subject in much greater depth.

## Putting some fun into kids earning their pocket money!

Our form is going to list three tasks that the child has to complete before they earn any pocket money. Each task will have a price to it, and how efficient the child is at carrying out their duties will determine how much they get at the end of the week. One task is to be done daily – if they miss a day, they lose money. Another task is to be done at least once weekly

## 76 Moving On from Computer Basics

and the final one is to choose from a list of favours that they accept to carry out when either Mum or Dad asks during that week – each time they do, they will earn more money.

1. On a new spreadsheet, list the tasks to be done and the prices paid for them. You can either make up your own or copy our examples as shown in Figure 56. Don't forget about formatting the Earnings columns to currency in the format menu.

|   | A | B | C | D | E | F | G |
|---|---|---|---|---|---|---|---|
| 1 |  |  |  |  |  |  |  |
| 2 | Daily Tasks | Earn | Weekly Task | Earn | Favours | Earn |  |
| 3 | Wash up after tea | £0.30 | Clean Bathrrom | £1.00 | Cup of tea | £0.20 |  |
| 4 | Dry up after tea | £0.30 | Clean Toilet | £1.00 | Shop errand | £0.20 |  |
| 5 | Take the Dog a walk | £0.25 | Hoover hall, stairs & Landing | £1.00 | Iron something | £0.20 |  |
| 6 | Tidy your own bedroom | £0.35 | Hoover living room | £1.00 | Run a bath | £0.20 |  |
| 7 |  |  | Dust living room | £1.00 |  |  |  |
| 8 |  |  | Cook a meal | £2.00 |  |  |  |
| 9 |  |  | Clean the car | £2.00 |  |  |  |
| 10 |  |  | Babysit | £3.00 |  |  |  |
| 11 |  |  |  |  |  |  |  |

Fig. 56. Some sample text.

2. At the bottom of the screen, click on Sheet 2. If you are not working with Excel, open a new worksheet (do not close the other one down). Highlight cells A2 to F3 and from the **format** menu choose **cells**. As shown earlier in the chapter, format these cells with a colour from the **patterns** tab and from the **alignment** tab, centre the horizontal and vertical text and merge the cells. From the **font** tab, change the font to bold and size 18 and click OK. In the **formula bar** at the top of the worksheet, type in Pocket Money Earnings.

3. Put in the rest of the titles, formatting the column widths and row heights appropriately, and the Earnings column to currency. Then select the rest of the form – in our example it was cells A4 to F16 – and give them a lighter colour. Your form should now look similar to Figure 57.

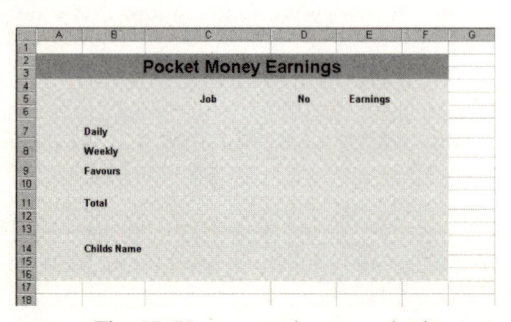

Fig. 57. How your chart may look.

4. Next, we need to put in the **combo** boxes that will list the jobs, but first we need to **name** the cells where the box will get its information from. Go back to Sheet 1 and highlight the cells A3 to A7 – this is the list of Daily Tasks starting at the first one, but ending with a blank row. Click on the **insert** menu and select **name**, then **define**. Type in 'DailyTasks' – all one word – and click OK. Now do the same for the other two columns, remembering to add in a blank line at the end with the highlighting. Name them 'WeeklyTasks' and 'Favours'.

5. We also need to link the Earnings column to the information. Highlight the cells A3 to B7 – this takes in the two columns of Daily Tasks and Earnings – once again adding that extra blank line at the bottom. Click on **insert**, **name** and **define** again and call this 'DailyEarnings' – all one word again, defining doesn't allow spaces. Do the same for the next two, calling them 'WeeklyEarnings' and 'FavourEarnings'. Now go and get yourself a cup of tea, you're doing well!

6. Now we are ready to start putting those boxes in. Return to Sheet 2 and from the **view** menu select **toolbars** and then **forms**. Another toolbox will have appeared: place your cursor over the fourth box down on the right – it should tell you it is a **combo** box. Select this, and then draw a box in cell C7 – the place where daily tasks are going to be listed. Right-click and choose **format control** as shown in Figure 58. In the new dialogue box, enter 'DailyTasks' as the **input range**, B20 as the **link cell** and four drop-down lines. The link cell just needs to be an empty cell somewhere on the same page as your chart. Now click away from it and test your box by clicking on the little arrow at the side. There will be your list 'Daily Tasks'.

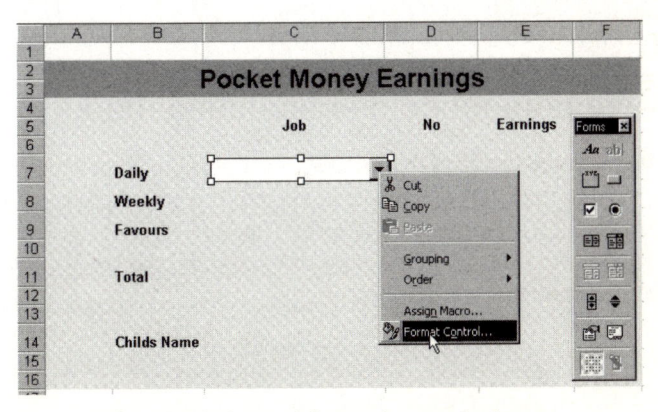

Fig. 58. Placing and formatting combo boxes.

7. In cell E7 we need to link the earnings to the number of times the task is carried out. Do this by clicking on the cell E7 and entering the formula:

    =INDEX(DailyEarnings,B20,2)*D7

    The index function finds its value from our defined name range called DailyEarnings, the value of which is determined from a link cell, the empty B20 cell again. The earnings are in the second column of the named range, hence the 2. The earning is then multiplied by the number of days the task was carried out as will be displayed in D7.

8. Click on the **spinner** tool in the **forms** toolbar (this is two below the combo box icon) and draw a box, filling half of the cell in D7. Right-click it and choose **format control**. This time we want the minimum value to be zero and the maximum value to be seven because this is going to show how many days of the week the task was carried out. The increments of one are fine. The cell link box is D7 because this is where we want our figure displayed – in the other half of the same cell. You will be able to click the up and down arrow of the spinner to alter the amount of days the task was carried out. Try it now.

9. We are now going to copy and paste the other boxes. Right-click on the combo box in cell C7 and select **copy**. Place your cursor in cell C8, right-click and choose **paste**. Right-click the box and choose **format control** to update the settings for the new box. Change the **input range** to WeeklyTasks and the **cell link** to C20. The number of drop-down lines can stay at four. Do the same again with cell C9, changing the next **input range** to Favours and **cell link** to D20. The spinner boxes can be copied and pasted too, remembering to right-click each one and change the cell link settings to D8 and D9. On the Favours one, the maximum value could be changed to 20.

10. Now copy and paste the Earnings box – what you are actually doing is copying the formula that is entered into this cell. At first you may get a VALUE message come up into the box. The formula needs changing which can be done in the formula bar at the top of the worksheet. The second needs to show:

    =INDEX(WeeklyEarnings,C20,2)*D8

    and the last one needs to read:

## Enhancing the Work of Spreadsheets 79

=INDEX(FavourEarnings,D20,2)*D9.

Finally, in the cell that you wish to display the amount of pocket money earned in one week, enter the formula:

=SUM(E7:E9)

This adds together all of the individual earnings from throughout the week.

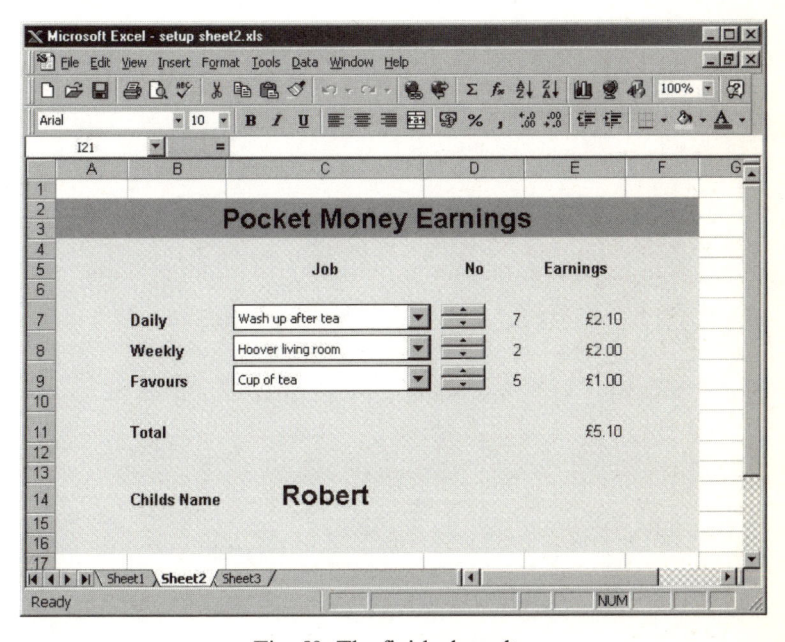

Fig. 59. The finished result.

We can now see from our form in Figure 59 that if Robert was to:

- wash the tea dishes every night for a week
- hoover the living room twice for Mum during the week
- make Dad five cups of tea during the week

he would earn himself more than £5 pocket money! As they get older, the figures on Sheet 1 can be adjusted accordingly.

## CASE STUDY

### Paula brightens up her financial report

Paula is the treasurer of the local school's Parent Teacher Association and has been looking for a way to brighten up her financial report. Having spent a few evenings learning the basics of a spreadsheet, she decides to create one in which to record her accounts for the previous year.

The practical exercise is good fun and Paula soon begins to find her feet. It takes her just a few evenings' work to produce a very impressive and neat summary. She can now use this information to produce a coloured chart so that others on the committee can see at a glance how the money raised has been used.

# 5

# Home Accounting with Finance Packages

## USING A FINANCE PROGRAM

We all need to keep track of our spending, especially when things are a little tight. A leading financier once said it's more important to know how broke you are, than how rich you are. Finance packages enable you to do this with the utmost accuracy providing a little effort is given to it. Some people may feel that this is a waste of time as we can get ministatements and balances from a hole-in-the-wall machine. However, having all your financial details available can be really useful for forward planning and budgeting. Let's see how it works.

Your finance program will be set up to mirror your household accounts. For example, you would create a bank account for each of your current and savings accounts, a credit card account for each of your credit cards and then liability and asset accounts for your loans and investments respectively. Each time you use these accounts, you must make an entry to reflect it in your computer accounts. Some payments, such as direct debits and other regular payments, credits and transfers, can be set to update automatically. Others, such as cash withdrawals and credit card transactions, have to be entered manually, say, once a week – copied from saved till receipts – to keep the accounts up to date. When statements arrive, these can be reconciled with the program thus highlighting any errors.

The program can be used a stage further if desired, to give a much greater level of detail for analysis. Each time an entry is made, a category can be assigned to the transaction. This information can then be used, over the course of time, to provide graphs and reports on where your money is being spent and to show you your true net worth at any given moment.

Some packages will also allow you to track VAT and other taxes, produce invoices and create logs for other things such as home inventories for insurance valuation. Throughout this chapter, we will use a program from Intuit called **Quicken**. **Microsoft Money** and others work in much the same way.

## SETTING UP A MONEY PROGRAM

When the program is installed, in order to begin entering your financial transactions, you have to set the accounts up. Quicken makes this easy for you by providing a wizard. Firstly, you are asked which type of account you need to set up, as seen in Figure 60. You are then asked to name your account, enter the balance either as it stands today, or from your last statement, and whether you need to track VAT. Credit card accounts can have their spending limit entered – the program will then warn you if you are approaching this limit.

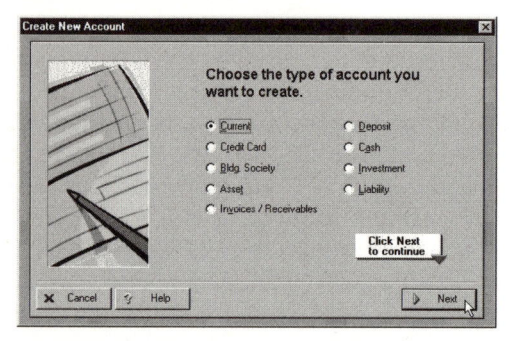

Fig. 60. Choosing an account to set up.

### Tracking your true net worth

If you want to track your true net worth, you need to set up counter-balancing accounts. For example, when setting up a liability account for a car loan, you would also need to set up an asset account to show the value of the car should you sell it. This is entirely optional – the program won't mind whether you bother or not, but if you don't, your net worth will never be 100 per cent accurate.

### Planning automatic regular payments

Once each of your accounts has been set up to mirror your real accounts, you then need to mirror the real standing orders, direct debits and transfers that you have with your bank. The beauty of a computerised home-accounting program is that, once these are set up, the computer never forgets about them – unlike us humans!

Quicken calls these **scheduled transactions**. As you can see from Figure 61, the dialogue box allows you to say:

- whether the transaction is a payment or receipt

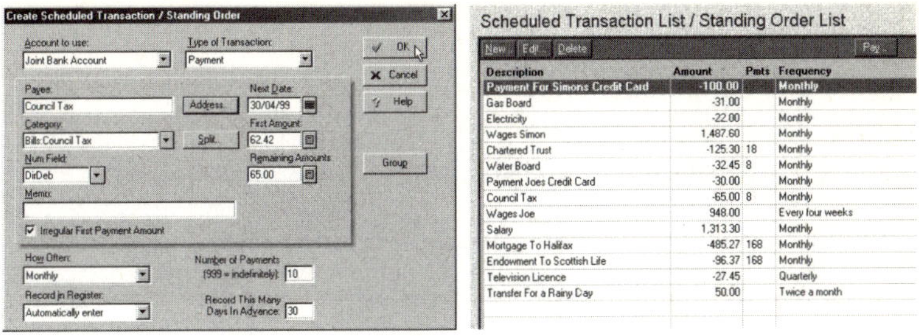

Fig. 61. The regular transaction boxes.

- which account the money should go from or be received into
- the identity of the payee
- the date the transaction should take place
- the number of days in advance to enter into your account
- how many payments or receipts there will be in total
- whether it should be entered automatically or manually
- how often the transaction takes place – weekly, monthly, one off, etc.
- what category the transaction should be tracked within
- how much the transactions amount to
- whether it is direct debit, standing order, transfer, switch, etc.

Once all the regular transactions have been set up, Quicken displays them in list form, also shown in Figure 61. Any one of them can be edited or deleted at any time simply by selecting the relevant transaction and using the buttons at the top.

*Knowing your balances*
Recording the date in advance of when a regular transaction is due to be executed can prevent you from thinking you have more money than you really do. For example, if you get paid on the last working day of each month, you could set Quicken to 'show' all the regular transactions on the following day – the first of the month. As seen in Figure 62, the direct debit to the gas board is actually paid on the 17th of the month – today is the 5th. It still shows the bill as being paid on the 17th, but it will be entered into the account on the 1st of the month – 16 days earlier – so that the ending balance of the joint account takes this payment into consideration.

| 03/04/99 | Cash D | Cash | | 50 | 00 | | | 240 | 11 |
|---|---|---|---|---|---|---|---|---|---|
| | | Cash | | | | | | | |
| 05/04/99 | | Tesco | | 85 | 26 | | | 154 | 85 |
| | | Groceries | | | | | | | |
| 08/04/99 | 101 | Petrol | | 28 | 54 | | | 126 | 31 |
| | | Motor:Fuel | | | | | | | |
| 17/04/99 | DirDeb | Gas Board | | 31 | 00 | | | 95 | 31 |
| | | Bills:Gas | | | | | | | |
| 05/04/99 | *Chq No* | *Payee* | | *Payment* | | *Deposit* | | | |
| | | *Category* | *Memo* | *Exp* | | Enter | Edit | Split | |
| | | | | | | **Ending Balance:** | | £95.31 | |

Fig. 62. Forward planning a transaction.

Many of us just look at the end amount on a statement and think 'gosh, have I got that much left?' and go out to spend it the following day because we haven't noticed that the mortgage hasn't yet been paid.

## Grouping your spends into categories

Quicken has an abundance of suggested categories, so many that it may put the small user off them. Do not let this deter you – it is easy to delete categories that are totally irrelevant to you. Have a look at this long list by selecting **categories/transfers** from the lists menu. Deleting has to be done one at a time, and sub-categories have to be deleted before the parent one can be got rid of, so it is a tedious job, but one that only has to be done once.

To create your own categories just click on **new** in the **category and transfer list** dialogue box as shown below. You can track any spending habit you like by giving it a description, an income or expense category of its own, or sub-categorising it under a parent group as shown in Figure 63. Once your list is set up, whenever you are entering a transac-

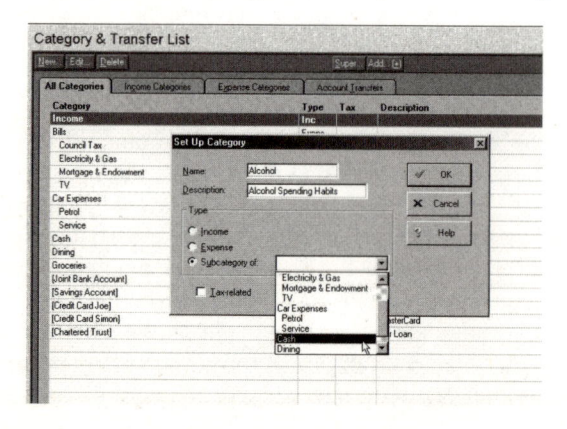

Fig. 63. Creating a new category.

tion, you will have the opportunity to categorise it into one of these groups. Then at a later date you can generate graphs and reports that will relate to your spending habits and probably give you a few shocks or surprises.

## KEEPING YOUR FINANCES UP TO DATE

Once you have completed the hard work of setting up a file, it doesn't take long to keep it up to date, but it does take a little discipline. You will need to:

- get into the habit of making sure you write on the cheque book stubs
- make sure you collect receipts for transactions on credit or debit card
- make a point of asking for a receipt at the hole-in-the-wall.

Once a week, or whatever suits you best, get all the receipts and chequebooks together and, using the information on them, enter all the transactions made since the last backup. Always back up any finance package to floppy disk immediately after entering any details – it only takes a few seconds and most money programs have an icon or an entry in the menu to automate the process. If you don't back up and your files get corrupted at a later date, you will have thrown away the receipts and this will leave 'holes' in your accounting.

### Entering transactions
One of the reasons we like Quicken is that the program is reasonably good in guiding you along.

1. When you open the program, a list of your accounts will be displayed in front of you – double-click on the one you wish to make an entry in.

2. The cursor will automatically be flashing at the first entry point, which is the date. Most of the fields have a tool at the right side – this will either be an arrow to open a list of possible choices, a calculator, or a calendar. On this first field it is a calendar. Click on it and select the date of the transaction.

3. Tab to the next field and select the arrow to list the choices of entry. This field lists the type of transaction – cheque, switch, cash withdrawal etc. It is optional and can be skipped if you wish.

4. Tab to the **payee** field. Type in to whom the transaction is applicable. If you have regular payees such as your grocery store or petrol station, you can add these to the memorised transaction group so that they can be selected from the list, thus eliminating the need to type it in each time.

5. Tab again and reach the **amount** field – make sure your cursor is positioned in the correct one. The first column is for a payment, the second for a deposit. If you filled in the optional field described in step three, the program will select the appropriate debit or credit column automatically. There is a calculator tool on the right side of the box.

6. The next field that the tab key takes you to is the **category**. This is optional but, as already mentioned, you can generate many graphs and reports using this information. This area is also used to transfer money from one account to another.

7. Finally, the **memo** field (again optional) is there for any additional notes that may be needed to clarify an entry.

8. When all the fields have been completed, the **enter** button is clicked on, recording the information and placing the cursor ready for the next transaction.

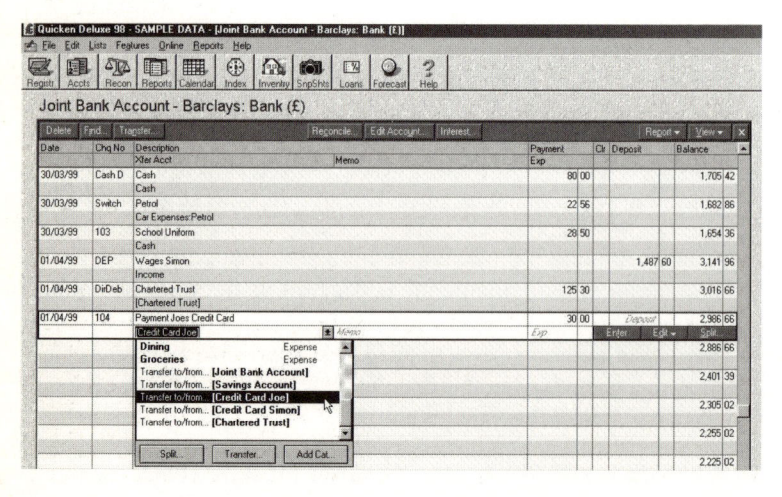

Fig. 64. Paying money to another account.

## Making a payment from one account to another (transfer of funds)

Making a payment from one account to another, such as when you write a cheque from your current account to pay the monthly payment to your credit card account, only takes one action in Quicken. Using the account from which you are debiting the money, enter the account to be credited in the **category** field as shown in Figure 64. This will then automatically make the credit entry in the other account.

## MAKING THE ACCOUNTS BALANCE

When you receive a statement from an account, open that account up in Quicken and click on **reconcile** to balance their figures with yours. The ending balance of your last statement will be showing, unless this is your first reconciliation, and you will need to enter the ending balance shown on your present statement. You can enter any interest either earned or charged in the box provided, click **OK** and begin to reconcile as shown in Figure 65.

Carefully go down your statement, ticking each transaction on the computer that your statement lists. The debits will be showing on the

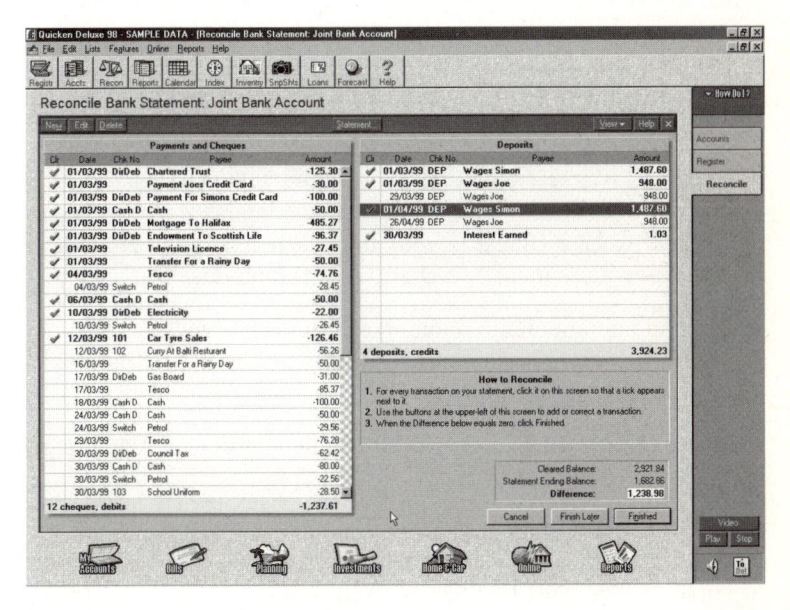

Fig. 65. Reconciling with a statement.

left side and the credits on the right. Your ultimate aim is to get the figure at the bottom right-hand corner to read £0.00 – which will mean that everything has balanced up.

### Adding entries that have been missed

During the reconciliation process, the statement may highlight a transaction that you can remember but have omitted to enter onto the computer. The account that is being reconciled can easily be reached by clicking on the **register** tab on the far right of the screen. This can be seen in Figure 65. The missing transaction can be entered and will automatically insert itself into the reconciliation update box faster than you can return.

If there are a number of discrepancies that need investigating, you can select the **finish later** or **cancel** button at the bottom of the screen. This will leave any unreconciled entries unmarked.

### Checking the income and outgoing balances

After a short while of running Quicken with categories, you can see where all your hard-earned cash is disappearing. There are many reports and graphs that can be generated – each of them can be customised to your own requirements. The options to choose from include:

- **Specific date ranges**. Name your exact dates or choose one of the pre-set configurations such as the previous quarter, or last year comparisons.

- **Include particular accounts**. Some accounts may be just for tracking purposes or may be to do with another member of your family and not to be included in your individual reports. Select exactly which accounts are to be included in which reports.

- Pick and choose which **categories** you wish to include. You may want to separate business from pleasure, or household necessities from extravagances!

- Other options allow you to **total** and **sub-total** in different ways, such as by month or by expense.

Once the report or graph is generated, parts of it can be double-clicked to find out more specific information relevant to that section. For example, in Figure 66, the food percentage was double-clicked to discover the breakdown of food cost in one particular month.

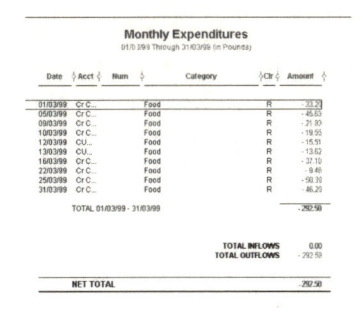

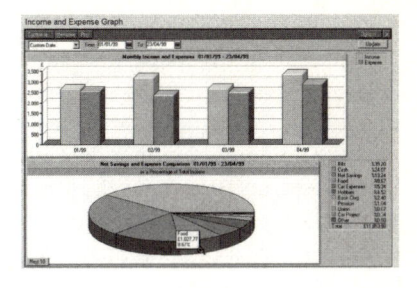

Fig. 66. A graphical display of spending habits.

## MORE EFFECTIVE MONEY MANAGERS

Most money programs can do quite a lot more than simply track transactions. Many allow integration with **online banking**, for example, which may enable the user to download transactions from their 'real' account into their computer account. Online banking facilities will sometimes include checking and updating share prices and other investment-related figures so that your balances can be updated whenever you require.

### Staying friendly with the tax man

If you need to track tax or VAT for business purposes, always check with your accountant's office before buying a program, to see which one will be acceptable to them. Quite often, accountants, and indeed the tax office, will be willing to receive your accounts direct from a computerised accounting package if it is approved, saving you hours of paperwork and therefore money.

There are now quite a few **self-assessment tax programs** available, including some that will allow data to be imported directly from your financial program. Some will display on the screen a replica of the forms that have to be sent to the tax office. Once you have filled them out, they can be printed, signed and popped straight into an envelope.

### Valuing your assets

One of the facilities of Quicken Deluxe is the **Home Inventory**. This allows you to list the contents of your house, room by room, and show an overall cost of replacing all your personal possessions should a disaster happen in your home. It is an ideal way of ensuring that your insurance cover is adequate.

## Calculating repayment costs

Another useful tool that many finance programs contain is the **loan calculator**. Providing you know the interest rate, you can enter details of a prospective loan amount and the period over which you would like to repay it. The program will then make an approximate calculation of the repayments. Alternatively, you can enter a repayment amount that you can afford and a calculation of a potential loan amount would be displayed, based on that repayment. Some will include calculators for mortgage terms and payments in addition.

## SUMMARY

To anyone who wants or needs to maintain an accurate view of their financial position, programs such as Quicken are a blessing. Once you are used to them, you will be amazed at just how beneficial they can be when planning anything that involves financial commitment.

If you run a **small business** from home, for which you do not keep separate bank accounts or credit cards, then they will make your life a lot easier. They can separate business receipts and purchases from personal ones enabling you, through the use of categories, to provide accurate indications of how well you are doing. If you ever want to borrow money, for expansion maybe, then your bank manager will need and appreciate this information.

Remember that finance is money, money is numbers and numbers are what computers are really good at.

## CASE STUDY

### Ted and Helen gain financial control

Ted and Helen always used to find it a struggle to meet large utility bills when they came through the letterbox. They changed over to paying each one of them by direct debit in an effort to get back on track. This was all very well, except there were so many of them – gas, electric, land line telephone, mobile telephone, water, council tax and TV licence – that when budgeting, they nearly always forgot to allow for at least one of them and ended up going overdrawn in their account.

Finally, Ted invested in a money program, and up to now – 6 months later – the couple have not been overdrawn on their account once. The computer 'pays' all bills on the same day that Ted's salary is credited, thus showing the true amount they have available to spend. The computer never forgets a bill, unlike Ted and Helen!

# 6
# Dealing with Databases

A database is simply a program that stores information input by the user. It is the way in which this information is input and stored, together with the way information can be retrieved, that makes these programs so powerful. Their structure can be quite complicated, especially if many complicated ways of retrieving the information are required. A business may operate many databases, for their stock controls, their staff management and maybe their statistical information. It may be that all of the databases are linked with each other so that the company can see at a glance which member of staff is producing the most work yet eating up the least amount of profits.

## THE DILEMMA OF DATABASES

To organise a database so that it provides in-depth information such as the above requires many hours to build and a lot of knowledge. If you need to learn this subject, then you will have to do a lot of research into what type of database would fulfil your needs and then concentrate on learning that package with the aid of a book dedicated to that program or perhaps a suitable training course.

For the convenience of the home user, many programs have wizards that will create a database geared to a particular chosen subject such as names and addresses or a music collection. This takes away the perplexing task of building it yourself. The wizard asks you some questions as to the type of fields you may require and the style you wish to apply and then does its best to give you a suitable database that is ready to use.

### Using databases created by the wizard

More often than not, the database that the wizard creates for you will be very near to your requirements, but some minor modification will probably be needed to make it just right. There may be additional fields required, or some that are not relevant and therefore need deleting – they may be in the wrong order. Certain areas may not be large enough to hold the information you need to enter – or may be too large for your needs.

Programs such as **Microsoft Access** are very good, but very complex. They are intended for business users who have high demands and although they do incorporate wizards for the uninitiated, if they require any amendments this can be quite a complex issue in itself.

There are simpler databases around, and if you just need to store your information, with perhaps a few little nifty extras like being able to **mail merge** and **print labels**, then we would suggest you pick one of these. **Microsoft Works** has an excellent database program that is easy to use and easy to amend. It's only downside, if you can call it that, is that it doesn't have some of the complex features of its sister program Access. This leaves you with a simpler, but nonetheless effective program.

### Explaining the structure basics

A database has two main working areas: **Design** mode, which is used for building and amending forms, and **Form** or **View** mode, which is where the database is used.

Building a database involves the following elements:

- creating areas called **fields** in which to enter information
- **formatting** and **labelling** the fields so that the user knows what entry is required
- **positioning** fields into a logical entry order
- applying **design** to make the records stylish, understandable and presentable
- **protecting** fields to prevent accidental change in design.

Using a database allows the following actions:

- **entering** information thus creating records
- **sorting** information into criteria for needs such as printing
- **viewing** information in list (multiple records) or form (single record) modes
- using **search facilities** to locate relevant information
- using **field** entries for **automatic processing**, such as **mail merge**.

The wizard, during creation, covers the building elements but you will need to use them if modifications are required. The user elements are all carried out by, well … you, the user!

**What we will achieve in this chapter**
As mentioned earlier, Microsoft Works is an excellent package that incorporates a word processor, spreadsheet and easy-to-use database. If you haven't got a copy of this program, it is available from most computer outlets at less than £50. We would recommend it as one of the easiest databases to achieve good results with, in the quickest possible time. We will use this program to show you how to set up a personal address database that will have the following information:

- names and addresses of your relatives and friends
- the names of their spouse and children
- birthday and anniversary dates to remember for each one
- telephone numbers with spaces for pagers, fax, e-mail addresses and mobiles
- a notes area to insert any additional information such as ideas for Christmas presents.

We will then show you how to sort information using an example of tasks you may wish to accomplish around Christmas such as:

- pick out all those people that need their card posted rather than delivered.
- from the selection above, print out the labels complete with addresses.
- Type one letter to all and utilise the database to send it to different people with the spaces filled in with the correct information on each copy.

## CREATING A DATABASE USING THE WIZARD

1. In the **Works Task Launcher** select **Common Tasks** and double-click on **Address Book**. You will be offered a choice of address books to suit home or business use. Select the first one, **Personal**, and click **Next**. The following screen tells you which fields the wizard will automatically include. Click on **Next** again.

2. Works allows you just a basic creation, or the choice of adding other components. It is best to add them at this stage – you can always remove any that aren't relevant later. Click on the **Additional Fields** tab and tick all relevant components as shown in Figure 67 and click OK.

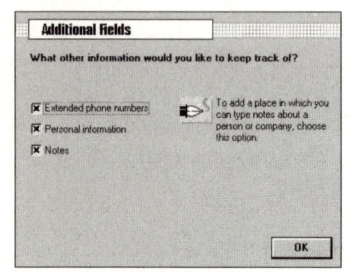

Fig. 67. Additional fields data.

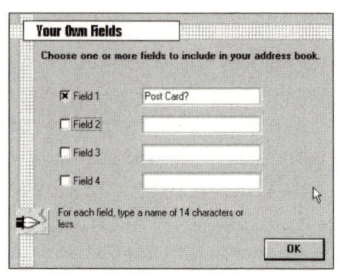

Fig. 68. Personalising additional fields.

3. In the **Your Own Fields** tab, as shown in Figure 68, select **Field 1** and type in 'Post Card?'. We will use this to show us a list of all cards that need to be posted and hence print the labels.

4. From the **Reports** tab, click on both the **Alphabetical** directory and the **Categorised** directory. These will help to give us printouts of all our entered information.

5. Finally click on the **Create it** button – you will be shown a quick summary of what you have chosen – click **Create Document** and away it goes building the database for you.

What you will have in front of you now is a database that is ready to use as shown in Figure 69. The first job is to save and name it. You can then access it from the existing documents tab of the Works task launcher in the future. To enter information, use the tab key or the direction arrows to move through the fields, but have a look through first and make any adjustments to the fields you feel are necessary in the following way.

## Making adjustments to the form

At the moment we are in **Form** mode – this mode is only used for entering or sorting information. To make adjustments we need to be in **Design** mode. Change to this by clicking on the **view** menu and selecting it from the list, or clicking on the relevant icon of the toolbar as seen in Figure 70.

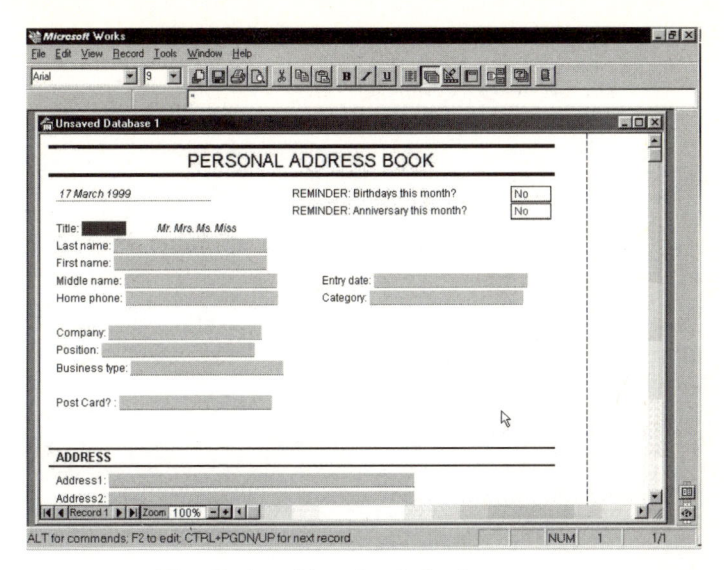

Fig. 69. An address book database screen.

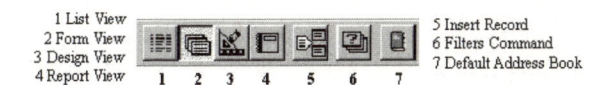

Fig. 70. Toolbar icons.

1 List View
2 Form View
3 Design View
4 Report View
5 Insert Record
6 Filters Command
7 Default Address Book

You will see that, in **Design** mode, all fields and labels have a dotted line around them. You can now change any part of your form such as the labels that describe what to enter in the fields, the field area itself or the form that they are sitting on.

### Removing unwanted fields

Whilst in Design mode, highlight the field you wish to remove and press delete on the keyboard – you will be warned that this cannot be reversed, click OK and it's gone. Do not delete the category field, as this will cause an error when we create a categorised report as chosen in the set up with the wizard. Also, you may be tempted to delete the title field, but this will be used when setting up the labels for posting cards. We have deleted the three business fields, the middle name and the entry date fields, which has created a bit of space on our form.

## Making the form more appealing
At the moment the form looks very bland with the white and grey shaded areas.

- To add a little style, click in any blank area of the form so that no particular field is selected and choose **shading** from the **format** menu. Choose a colour for your form from the **foreground colour box**.
- Change the **colour of the field areas** too by right-clicking on them and selecting **shading**. Multiple fields can be selected by holding down the Ctrl key while selecting them.
- By selecting **Font** and **Style** from the menu you can change the type of font or the size it will be when entered. The field area will automatically adjust to accommodate the new size of font.
- **Label styling** can be changed in the same way as fields.
- Each field and its label can be **repositioned** by holding the mouse button down while selected. Drag it around to a new position.
- **Field lengths** can be adjusted by selecting and using the resize handles around the outside of the box.

Our form now looks a lot more appealing, as seen in Figure 71, where we have begun entering our first record.

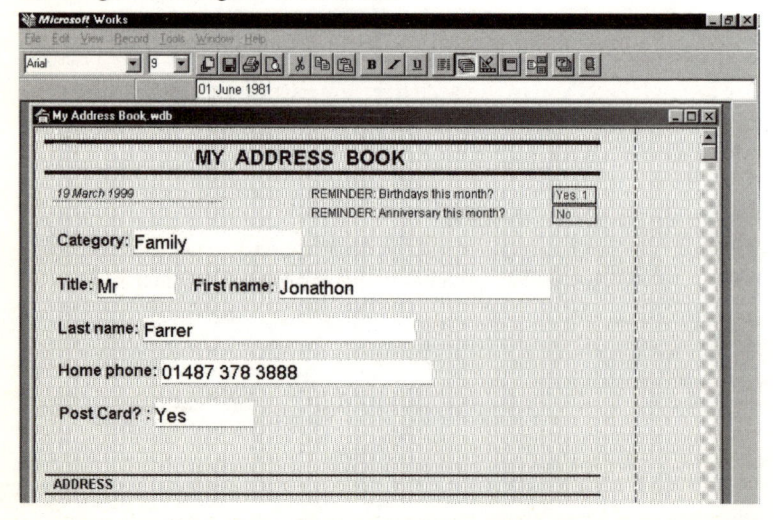

Fig. 71. The more stylish appearance.

## Changing the tab order

To make entries flow in a different order: still in Design mode, select **tab order** from the **format** menu. We are shown a list, which is how the order is placed at the moment. Move the fields into the correct order by selecting the relevant one and using the up and down buttons to reposition it. In Figure 72 we have selected the first name field: pressing the up button will put it into its correct place.

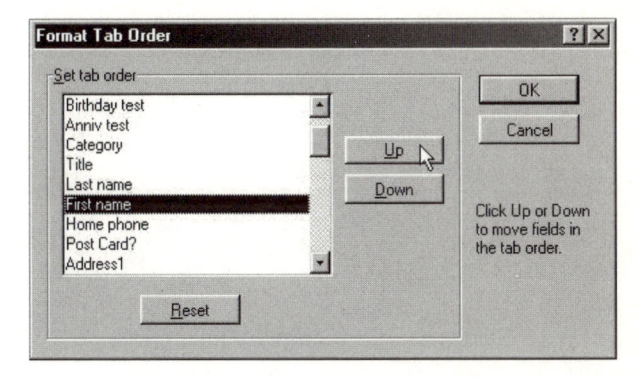

Fig. 72. Changing the tab order.

Now, switch back into form view, save your database again and begin entering in the information about your relatives and friends. We can then proceed to the next stage.

## USING REPORTS AND PICKING OUT RECORDS

In our example address book, we have entered ten fictitious names and addresses with a category of either friend or family. We can now click on the **report** icon on the toolbar to view and print a list of all the people we have in our database.

At first we are shown a template: this is the design for the database report that the wizard created at the beginning. It has references to the fields it is going to display. This can be changed quite easily but we will not cover that subject in this chapter.

Click on the **print preview** icon to see how the report will print the list. It will list all the family in one category and all friends in another. If you can see an **ERR** on your sheet, it is probably because you have deleted one of the fields that the report was expecting to read from. Have a look back at the report template, see if you can find the reference to the deleted field and remove it. The report layout can be altered to suit by adjusting the template's entries – check out the help files for more information on this.

### Picking out particular records

It is easy to pick out particular records with Works. Let's go back to our example of creating a list of all people to whom we need to post a Christmas card.

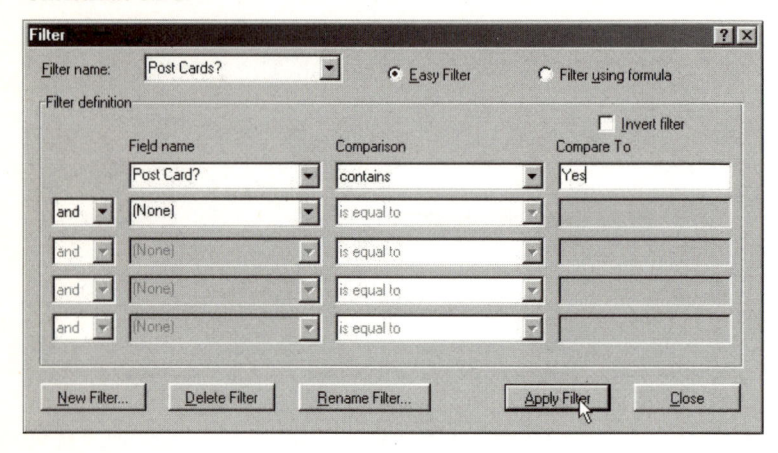

Fig. 73. Entering filter criteria.

- First click on the **Filters** command icon and name the filter '*Post Card?*'.

- In the dialogue box, as seen in Figure 73, we have to enter our criteria.

This example is fairly straightforward. We want to know if the field name *Post Card?* contains the word '*Yes*' – if so, list it. When we click on **apply filter**, the database will show us all records that fulfil the criterion. Records that don't match this criterion will be hidden from view. Ensure that **List View** is selected to see all of these at a glance.

More than one criterion can be applied at the same time. For example, we could have asked it to show us only those records that contained the words '*Yes*' in the *Post Card* field and which were in the category *Friend*. Then we could just pick up our box of Christmas cards, write them all out, pop them in the envelopes and post. Later we could tell the filter we now want all *Family* categories shown and print out the list of special cards we need to buy for our family.

### Marking records for future selection

We could have gone straight to the labelling process with our selected files showing, but we will take it one step further to explain a little about the marking of records. Down the left side of the screen in **List View** there are boxes that can be ticked to mark records. If you mark all the records that need their cards posting, then from the **Records** menu, select **Show/All records** – the previously hidden records will now be in view again but without a mark, as seen in Figure 74. Save the database and we will now take you through printing your labels.

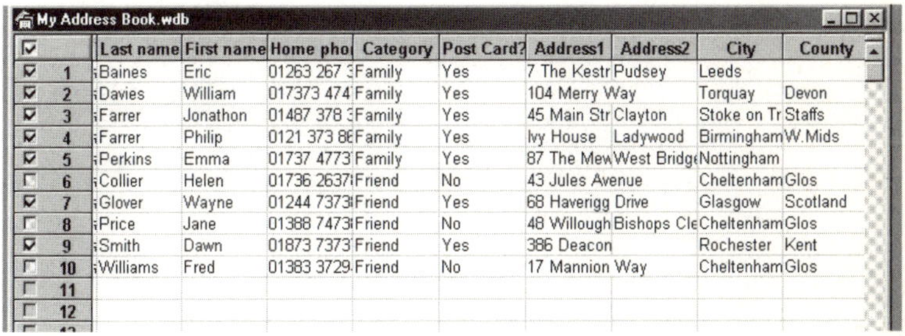


| ☑ | | Last name | First name | Home pho | Category | Post Card? | Address1 | Address2 | City | County |
|---|---|---|---|---|---|---|---|---|---|---|
| ☑ | 1 | Baines | Eric | 01263 267 3 | Family | Yes | 7 The Kestr | Pudsey | Leeds | |
| ☑ | 2 | Davies | William | 017373 474 | Family | Yes | 104 Merry Way | | Torquay | Devon |
| ☑ | 3 | Farrer | Jonathon | 01487 378 3 | Family | Yes | 45 Main Str | Clayton | Stoke on Tr | Staffs |
| ☑ | 4 | Farrer | Philip | 0121 373 86 | Family | Yes | Ivy House | Ladywood | Birmingham | W.Mids |
| ☑ | 5 | Perkins | Emma | 01737 4773 | Family | Yes | 87 The Mew | West Bridge | Nottingham | |
| ☐ | 6 | Collier | Helen | 01736 2637 | Friend | No | 43 Jules Avenue | | Cheltenham | Glos |
| ☑ | 7 | Glover | Wayne | 01244 7373 | Friend | Yes | 68 Haverigg Drive | | Glasgow | Scotland |
| ☐ | 8 | Price | Jane | 01388 7473 | Friend | No | 48 Willough | Bishops Cle | Cheltenham | Glos |
| ☑ | 9 | Smith | Dawn | 01873 7373 | Friend | Yes | 386 Deacon | | Rochester | Kent |
| ☐ | 10 | Williams | Fred | 01383 3729 | Friend | No | 17 Mannion Way | | Cheltenham | Glos |
| ☐ | 11 | | | | | | | | | |
| ☐ | 12 | | | | | | | | | |

Fig. 74. A display of records -- some marked.

## PRODUCING LABELS FROM SELECTED RECORDS

With your database open, go to the **Tools** menu and select **Labels**. The task wizard takes you through a very thorough step-by-step process with questioning such as:

1. **What size labels will you be using**? There is a comprehensive list for you to choose from. If the size of your label happens not to be listed, you can create a custom size by entering in the relevant dimensions.

2. **Which database records do you want to print**? Here you have the choice of selecting all the records in the chosen database, current records visible, marked records or named filtered records.

3. **Which fields do you want on your label**? This is the clever bit. You select a field you need from the list and click the **Add Field** button after each one – this list shows all the fields in your chosen database. The way in which you place them is how they will be displayed on the label. As you will see in Figure 75, we chose the title, first name and last name fields to be on the same line, then used a new line for each of the address fields.

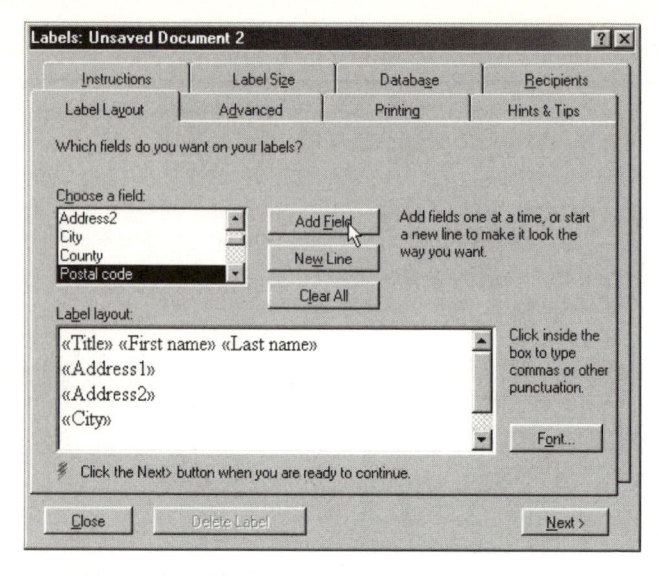

Fig. 75. Setting up address labels.

4. **Finally you are given the printing options**. Select how many copies you require then choose **preview** to check the layout. Ensure your labels are loaded into your printer tray and click on **Print**.

### Saving the label for future use

If you do not choose to print from the preview screen, the program leaves the label fields set up in a word processing document. This is common, as it is actually the word processing application that prints the labels – it just uses the database to provide the information. You can save the label as a separate document and open it at any time in the future. When you go to preview, it will again look up the information from the relevant database.

If your saved label included marked records and subsequent changes to your database affected these records, then these changes will be reflected next time you open the label file.

### SAVING TIME WITH MAIL MERGE

Mail merge is where you can type a letter, just one letter, but print as many copies as you like with each separate copy having different details taken from individual records in the database. For example, you could start your letter with 'Dear...' and then insert the database field that contains the first name of each record. Thus, your first letter will read 'Dear Julie', your second letter 'Dear Robert' and so on.

## How it is done
In our example we will create a letter in the Microsoft Works word processor and list all the birthdays of our family and friends – asking to be updated on any that are missing or incorrect.

1. Prepare the letter as you would normally, except when you get to a place where you need to retrieve information from the database, go to the **Insert** menu and choose **Database Field**.
2. In the box given, click on the **Use a different database** button and select your database.

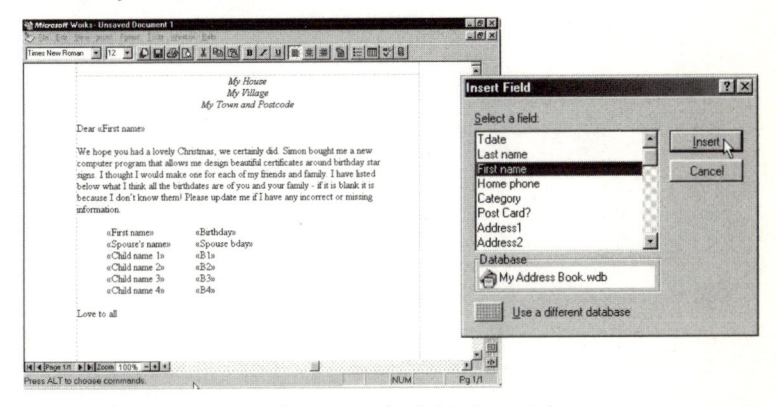

Fig. 76. Using database fields in mail merge.

3. Now you will see the list of fields inside that database as shown in Figure 76. Select the one that you require and click **Insert**. When you are finished your letter should look something like ours.
4. Click on **print preview** and Works will tell you it will preview all records. Click OK and view each record in turn by clicking on **Next**. The relevant information will have been entered automatically as shown in Figure 77 – ready for you to click on the **Print** button.

As you will appreciate by now, the subject of databases can be quite complex, but need not be if your requirements are straightforward. Our advice is the same here as with other programs: use it and experiment with it and you will soon get a feel for it.

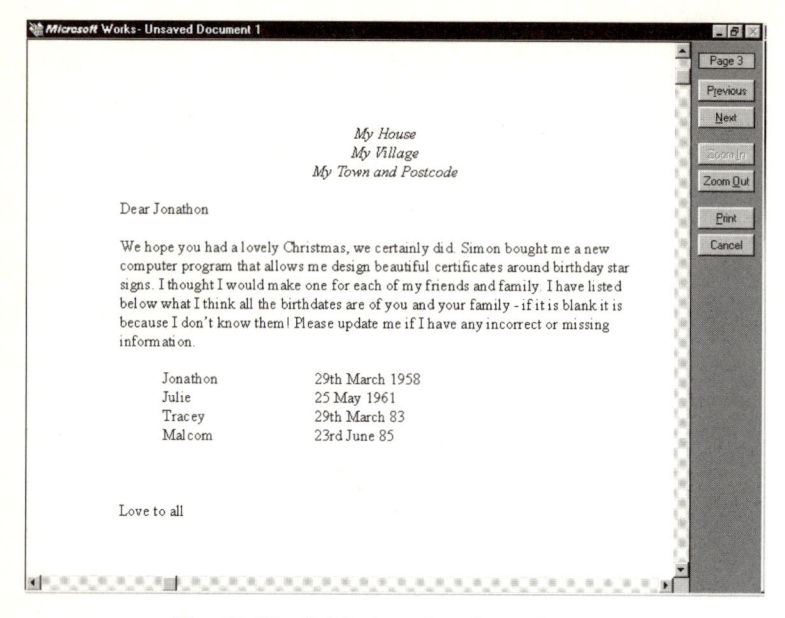

```
                          My House
                         My Village
                    My Town and Postcode

    Dear Jonathon

    We hope you had a lovely Christmas, we certainly did. Simon bought me a new
    computer program that allows me design beautiful certificates around birthday star
    signs. I thought I would make one for each of my friends and family. I have listed
    below what I think all the birthdates are of you and your family - if it is blank it is
    because I don't know them! Please update me if I have any incorrect or missing
    information.

        Jonathon           29th March 1958
        Julie              25 May 1961
        Tracey             29th March 83
        Malcom             23rd June 85


    Love to all
```

Fig. 77. The finished results of a mail merge.

## CASE STUDY

### Chris improves his track record

Chris is a part-time disk jockey and has a huge array of records and CDs. Often he is asked to prepare music to run along a particular theme such as music from the 70s, jazz or only tracks with titles beginning with the letter 'C'. Sometimes it can be a nightmare trying to sort them all out.

Having found out how to use a database, Chris can now produce a list of tracks, sorted and printed ready for the customer's approval in just a few minutes. Unfortunately the computer can't dig through the piles of boxes, pulling them out for him, but then it's not a perfect world!

# 7

# More Wonders of the Web

Going on the Internet or finding things on the web ('surfing' as some people say) needs a correctly configured **modem** inside your computer, a **telephone line** and some **software** that allows access.

## CONNECTING TO THE INTERNET
### What is an ISP?
An **Internet Service Provider** (ISP) allows you to connect to their computer servers via your modem and telephone line. In doing this you will be using their equipment, enabling you to access information found on the net. They normally provide the necessary software to load onto your computer. This will include a suitable **browser** for viewing the pages if one is needed. Examples of browsers are Microsoft's Internet Explorer or Netscape's Navigator. The software will also configure the settings required, such as the relevant telephone number to dial and details of the server names that you may want to connect to in order to be able to use e-mail and newsgroups, etc.

### Choosing an ISP
There are hundreds of ISPs to choose from. At the time of writing, popular names that provide their software on many magazine covers are AOL and CompuServe – their subscriptions are around £5–£10 per month. Freeserve, available from Dixons and PC World, doesn't cost the customer a penny for subscribing; the only cost of being on the Internet is your own telephone bill. British Telecom, Virgin and many other ISPs have now seen the light and have stopped charging users for their net time (don't forget the phone bill though!).

### Addressing your identity
When subscribing with an ISP, you choose a name that will identify yourself. The way this identity is made up varies according to the provider. It is with this identity that your e-mail address, user name and provider details are set up.

Signing up to your chosen ISP may be a lengthy procedure, so be prepared to set aside a quiet hour to complete setting up your system.

*Choosing a name*
If you run a business and intend creating a web page, a little strategy can be used when creating an identity. For example, if your business name is Fast Crafts, an identity such as staff@fastcrafts.freeserve.co.uk could be created

- The identity as a whole would be your **e-mail address**.
- If **multiple e-mail addresses** are allowed with your chosen provider, the name before the @ could be substituted with individual staff names such as joebloggs@fastcrafts.freeserve.co.uk.
- Your **username** usually consists of everything after the @.
- Some providers use the username as an address to your personal **web space**. So people would type in http://www.fastcrafts.freeserve.co.uk to see your web page.
- The *freeserve.co.uk* part identifies your **provider**.

During the sign up procedure, your provider will normally have configured your computer settings to go directly to their home page, this is their address. If you have an Internet Explorer icon on your desktop, right-click on this and select properties to see what the home page address is.

### How do I connect?
Double-click on your provider's icon. A **dial-up connection box** will appear on your screen such as the one in Figure 78, showing the connection details. Enter your **password** – if you don't want to enter this every time, check the **Save Password** box and the connection will automatically fill this entry in each time for you. Take note, if you do check this option, anyone who has access to your computer will be able to log on to the net. It is ideal if it is only you who will use the system, but watch the kids!

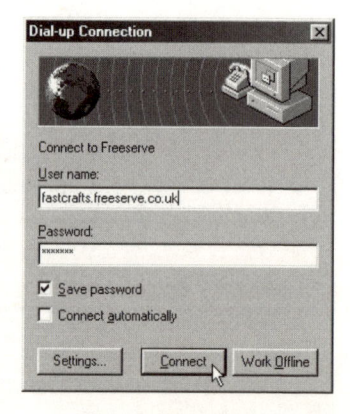

Fig. 78. The dial-up connection box.

Next, click on the **connect** button. You will hear a few noises as the modem dials the number. Once a successful connection has been gained, the home page will be displayed and the small icon resembling two telephones will be showing on the right side of the taskbar.

## FINDING WHAT YOU ARE LOOKING FOR

The home page will have a variety of topics for you to click on. Clicking on **Sport**, for example, will take you to another page that has a breakdown of different types of sport. Click on your choice, such as **Football**, and this may take you to yet another page giving you a choice of teams, international news, or results, etc. It can seem as if these choices go on for ever. Choices that you click on to take you to another page are known as **links**.

If you are looking for something specific, there are quicker ways to get nearer the information, without having to go through all that rigmarole.

### Going direct to the site

You may have seen on the television and many other places – find us at 'www.wherever.thisthat.andother'. This '**domain name**' as it is known, can be typed in at the address bar, usually found at the top of the screen as seen in Figure 79. Type in the name after the http:// and press the enter key to go direct to that site.

Fig. 79. The address bar.

### But it didn't work!

If you receive an error page or an 'unable to retrieve' message, there could be a number of reasons. The name has to be typed exactly correct. It could be compared to your telephone number – one wrong digit and you will be talking to somebody else. This domain name is converted into an IP address (Internet Protocol) which consists of four lots of numbers between 0 and 255. It is this IP address that identifies each computer on the net. The site you are trying to reach may be 194.62.58.102, but if you have typed one incorrect letter, the conversion process will have failed. Check the following:

- Does the site still exist?
- Has the address changed?

- Have you mistyped the address? It needs to be exactly right, including capital and small letters. Unfortunately the web is **case sensitive**.
- Does http://www. precede your address?
- Have you included the co.uk or .com if there is one?
- Have you entered the correct forward slashes (/) not backslashes (\)?
- Are you logged on to your ISP?
- Are you entering an address with @ in it. This is an e-mail address, not a web address.

### Using a search engine

If you do not know the specific address of a web site that you are interested in, but wish to find out what sites may contain the information you are looking for, try using a **search engine**.

A search engine could be compared to a telephone directory, but online and automated. You give a description of what you wish to look for and it will list relevant sites that it is aware of containing this description. There are many search engines on the net and they vary on how they look up information. Some put the content of a site into a category and list it accordingly; others take keywords from a site and will list it when these keywords are part of the description.

Web site creators submit their **URL** –the technical name for a web address – to a search engine for listing. So, as with the *Yellow Pages*, if a business doesn't advertise, it will probably not be found – except by recommendation.

### How it looks for requested information

Let's say a web site was created with information about greyhound dog breeding. In the submission to a search engine, the creator would give a short description about the site or ensure the page title accurately describes its content, and include possible **keywords** that people may enter to retrieve it. Keywords may include descriptions such as dogs, breeding, greyhounds, plus individual varieties of breeds or particular breeder's names.

When people type these keywords into a search engine as part of their description, the engine looks up sites that meet the criteria. When a match is found, the site will be one of many listed and will contain a link that can be clicked on to go straight to it. The description, or the first line or two of the pages, will be shown with the listing, so that people can decide if this is in fact the type of information that they may be searching for.

Unfortunately, some web sites, in order to attract your attention, will submit a bit of a red herring to the search engine. On a recent enquiry for information about the television show *Friends*, we typed in 'TV Series Friends' and got a listing for a transvestite dating agency. Still, that's life on the net – full of surprises!

### Finding a search engine

1. Your ISP will usually provide quick access to at least one search engine. In Figure 80, the right pane shows the home page of Freeserve ISP. A search keyword entered into the indicated box takes the user direct to the Lycos search engine and its retrieved sites.

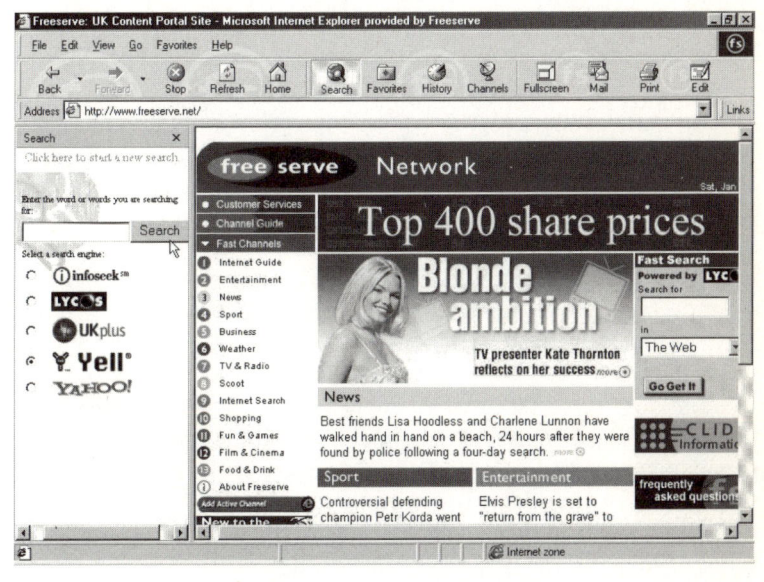

Fig. 80. Selecting a search engine.

2. Clicking on the **Search** button of the **Internet Explorer** browser opened the left pane. A keyword entered into this box will retrieve site URLs using the selected search engine. If you don't find what you're looking for on one search engine, try another, because they will often come up with different sites.

3. Type in the **URL address** of the relevant search engine in the address box.

## Some URLs of search engines for you to try

*General purpose and category search engines*

| | |
|---|---|
| AltaVista | http://www.altavista.com |
| Lycos | http://www.lycos.co.uk |
| Excite | http://www.excite.co.uk |
| Ask Jeeves | http://www.aj.com |
| Yahoo! | http://www.yahoo.co.uk |

*Specialists*

| | |
|---|---|
| Encarta | http://encarta.msn.com – Microsoft's online encyclopaedia |
| Yell | http://www.yell.co.uk – UK-based business directory |
| NewsLinx | http://www.newslinx.com – news-based searches |
| LookSmart | http://www.looksmart.com – graphical arts resources |
| Intelihealth | http://www.intelihealth.com – medical and health orientated |
| GeoCities | http://www.geocities.com – online community based |

## Using portals and keywords

Most search engines have a menu system to assist you with your search – these are sometimes referred to as a **portal**. All search sites have a box in which you enter keywords to describe what you are searching for. The more descriptive you can be, the more your search will be narrowed down to an exact match – the more vague you are, the more choices you may get.

Using a mixture of the two search methods is often the best idea. For example, if you wish to find out about a pop group's fan club, use the menu system first to enter the music category, then to enter the pop world category. Once here, you can type the name of the band into the search box and the engine will only check out that field of possible returns, making the search quicker and more defined.

## How to be even more precise

Most search engines have ways of enabling you to be even more precise with your search. Check out their help pages to find individual differences. For example:

- To find recipes for apple pie – typing in the two words would retrieve sites that have the word apple and/or the word pie in them. To narrow it down, you can tell the search engine that it **must have** both words. To do this put a **plus sign** at the beginning of the word (i.e. +apple +pie), this will only return links that have both words associated.

- Similarly, you can use the **minus sign** to eliminate unwanted links i.e. Monty –Python would return pages with the word Monty, but not Monty Python.

- **Quotation marks** can be used around phrases or words. This will retrieve web sites that have the wording within their site that is inside the quotation marks. This is useful for finding very specific information such as authors' books or popular sayings.

## DOWNLOADING FROM THE INTERNET

The Internet has many uses, including the availability of educational material, e-mail, chatting to people all over the world, being able to shop for unusual or cheaper products as well as fun and games, checking out train timetables, weather forecasts and road conditions – the list is endless. Downloading things from the Internet can get you out of many sticky situations. For example:

- You are near completing an important portfolio for your boss but could do with a **photograph** or **picture** to explain your project – find it on the net and download it.

- You have heard about a **shareware program** that sounds exactly what you're after but you can't find it anywhere (unless you're willing to pay £10 postage!). Download it from the net.

- You have just found out that your **printer drivers** conflict with your new scanner. You are told there is an updated driver available that corrects this if you are willing to send yet another £10 postage, when they will be forwarded on to you. Download them from the net.

### Grabbing a picture

Most pictures on the net can be saved for your own use. In Figure 81 the Interflora site had the perfect picture needed for a garden newsletter about growing flowers for cutting. Right-click on the object and from the menu choose **Save picture as**... The familiar dialogue box will appear giving you a chance to tell it where it should be saved. It is wise to create a new folder, perhaps called *Web Downloads*, to save all your

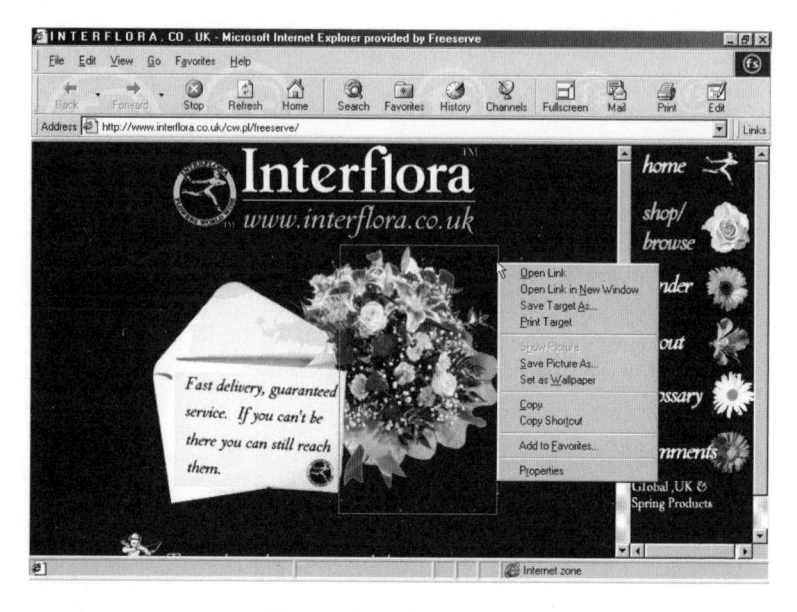

Fig. 81. Grabbing a picture.

downloads in, otherwise they are saved in the Temporary Internet Files folder along with hundreds of other cached files. It can take an age to find them afterwards.

Once you have saved it, you can view it from your photo-editing package and make the necessary adjustments as described in our second chapter, or you can insert it directly into your desktop publishing or word processing document using the relevant commands.

## Explaining an FTP site

FTP stands for **File Transfer Protocol**. An FTP site is a place on the Internet where you can browse for particular items such as shareware programs, lyrics to your favourite song or drivers for your computer, etc. When you have found what you're looking for, you can transfer the item from their computer to your own – download it. It could be compared to a massive library that stocks all sorts – when someone takes something away, it is automatically replaced for another person to see.

You can use special FTP programs to connect to sites and download items, but many web pages offer automatic downloads that save you the bother of using them. One site that is a good example of this is www.shareware.com as seen in Figure 82. Others will include places such as printer manufacturer sites and sound card manufacturer sites – they will have a page that allows you to download their latest drivers.

Fig. 82. A download site.

## So how do I actually download something?

1. Double-click on the file that you want.
2. A box will appear asking 'Do you wish to save the file to disk?'. Select **Yes**.
3. Select the folder to save the file into and click OK.

Your file will now begin downloading. How long this takes depends on how big the file is. If it is relatively small in size, such as a driver or a sound file, it may only take a few seconds or a minute or two. Programs can vary in size enormously – a trial version of a program that is 20 megabytes or so may take up to an hour or more to download. The download dialogue box will normally give you some indication of its progress in predicted time to completion.

You can carry on surfing the net while the downloading process carries on in the background. The only thing that will stop the download is if you disconnect from the Internet. Once it is complete it is available for use immediately and can be treated just as any other file on your system.

- Check the site where you downloaded from for any instructions on what to do with the file once it is transferred.
- If there do not appear to be any instructions, check for a **readme.txt** that may have accompanied the file.
- If you cannot find any instructions, it may be that the file itself needs double-clicking to either execute it or unzip it.

## BUILDING AND PUBLISHING A WEB PAGE

There are many programs available for building your own web page. Popular programs such as **Microsoft Word** and **Publisher** also allow you to design a web page as if you were designing an ordinary flyer and then convert the creation to the **HTML** code that is required for displaying web pages. Our examples are using Microsoft Publisher 98.

We are not going to teach you to build a web page here – there would be so many options that we would need a complete book to explain it rather than part of a chapter. What we will explain is some of the differences between a web page file and an ordinary word processing or desktop publishing file and the considerations you need to bear in mind when building a web page. This knowledge will benefit you immensely if you decide to have a go at building or designing a page, or if you wish to create a page, but don't wish to learn anything about HTML code or web page building programs.

We will then briefly go into publishing your page, which is the process of transferring your creation onto the ISP's server so that people can view your site. This involves using an FTP (file transfer protocol) program and understanding the settings you need to know.

### Finding your web space

Most ISPs allow you a certain amount of free web space on their server. This can be used to display whatever you like. Some people advertise their business, or set up fan club news for their favourite person or it may be that you have a hobby, such as photography, and want to display your latest pictures to the world.

You may have to 'create' your web space before being able to use it. Check out the **help files** from your ISP's home page. This is normally a simple case of typing in your web space address. Accessing the space for the first time **creates** the space and URL (address). It really is very important to ensure you have read the help files and do what is required in the correct order, otherwise it could cause you much frustration in the initial set-up.

### Understanding the index file

Your ISP may need you to call your opening page by a certain name – this should be listed in their help files. It will normally be **index** or **default**, but look closely because it may be important whether the first letter is a capital or small letter and the extension may need to be either **.htm** or **.html**.

This opening page, if called index, does not mean that it has to be that

– an index – it is simply the first page that will automatically be shown when somebody accesses your site. If none of your files that make up your web site creation have this name, the server will not understand which page to display first.

Your web site can consist of only one page if you wish. Any further pages that you add can be named whatever you like as long as the opening page is named accordingly. Your viewers will access these further pages via links from your index page.

### Sizing your page
When creating your site you are not limited to page sizes such as A4 or B5 – you could have almost any size within reason, but bear in mind the people who will be viewing it. If your page is too wide, it may be fine when viewing it on a 19-inch screen. But someone who has a 14-inch screen will have to use the bottom scroll bar to view either side of your page, which can be annoying and may lose their interest. **Microsoft Publisher** has an easy web page set-up that has **default**, **wide** and **custom** settings as shown in Figure 83.

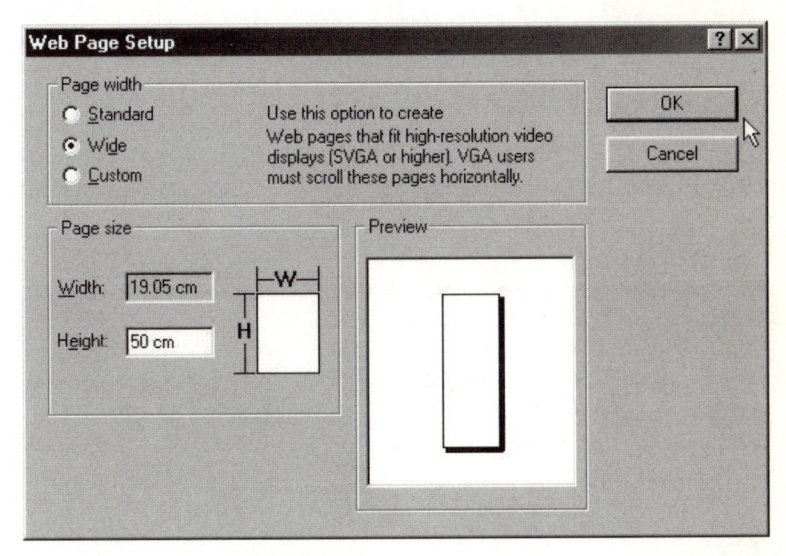

Fig. 83. Setting the page size.

Having one long page isn't always a good idea. Although links can be dotted around the page that immediately skip the viewer from one part to another, it is perhaps more interesting to have multiple pages with a topic on each.

## Using graphics
Each time a person accesses a web page, the information it contains is transferred to his or her own computer **cache memory** for viewing. Graphics can be large files and take the longest to download. When inserting graphics, always use a compressed file type such as **gifs** or **jpegs**. More information on the differences and what these file types are can be found in Chapter 2.

You may have already come across some web sites that seem to take an age to display their contents. How many times have you thought you can't be bothered to wait, and gone off elsewhere on your surf! This is the danger of using too many graphics, or indeed only a few, but of high detail. This applies not only to photographs or clipart but to animated items too.

## Laying out your design
Unlike a desktop publisher, take a little care not to overlap pictures and text. On conversion to **html** code, a piece of text that is too close to a graphic will be seen as a complete graphic and therefore take longer to view. If a graphic needs to be close to text, create each item in its own frame then position them accordingly. In Figure 84 the title is one piece of text, the picture stands on its own and each piece of text either side of the picture is also in its own frame. This way they can be close together, but will not be grouped as one large picture.

Fig. 84. Keeping frames apart.

## Adding a hyperlink

Your viewers will need to get from one page to another on your site – and back again – so don't forget to put in the **hyperlink** that allows them to do this. A hyperlink is one of those underlined pieces of text. It has an instruction attached to it so that, when it is clicked on, it takes the viewer to another area that contains subject matter referred to in the link. Enter the text and format it, then select a relevant word or phrase and choose **hyperlink** from the **Insert** menu. You can create a hyperlink to:

- **another web site address** by entering the http://information
- **an e-mail account** by entering the appropriate address
- **another page** on your own web site as seen in Figure 85
- **a file** on your hard disk by entering the path to this file.

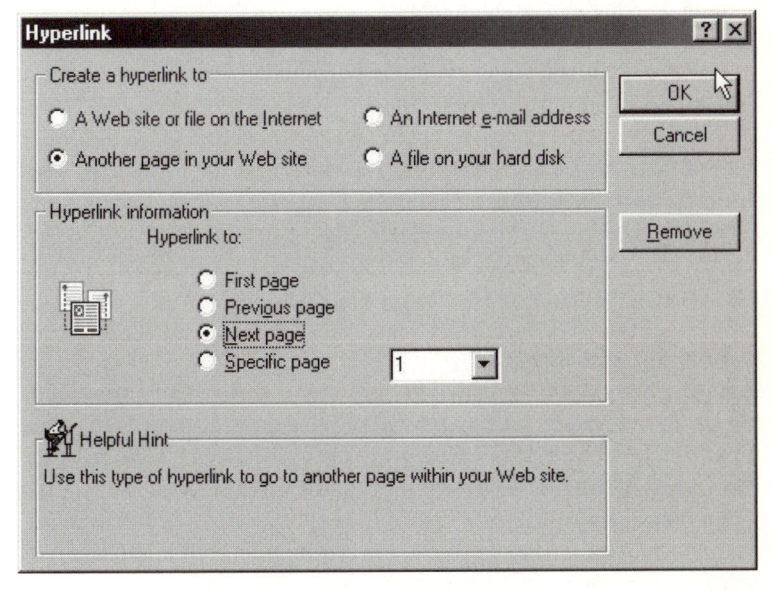

Fig. 85. Creating a hyperlink.

To recap, keep your index (first) page brief and to the point and don't make it too fancy. By doing this it will download faster and encourage viewers to explore the links.

### Preparing for publishing on the web

Microsoft Publisher has a **design checker** to make sure you have not overlooked anything on your web site. It can be found in the **Tools** menu and checks for things such as empty frames, frames that aren't large enough for the text that is in them and overlapping of text and graphics, amongst many other faults. If there is a problem, a description box will bring it to your attention as shown in Figure 86.

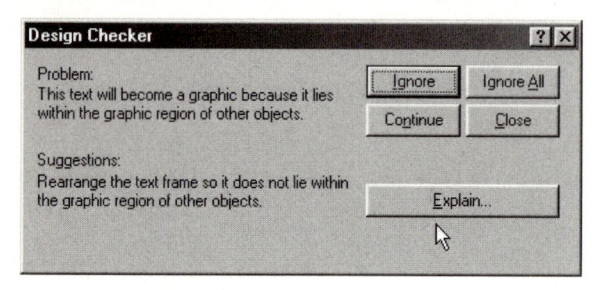

Fig. 86. Checking for design faults.

When everything seems fine, there is yet another check that Publisher allows: this is to click on **Web Site Preview** from the **File** menu. This opens the **Internet browser** and displays your site as if you were viewing for real on the Internet. You can check that the hyperlinks work and that it looks how you intended it to look. This will all happen offline and will not actually log you on to the net.

### Publishing your files

Publisher has its own simplified program for transferring files (**uploading**) from your computer to your ISP's. It has its limitations but is ideal for a beginner. The uploading program is installed as an addition but is then accessed from the **File** menu within the main program.

Individual FTP programs can be found on the cover of Internet magazines or from the net available for downloading, free of charge, at places such as **www.ipswitch.com**. FTP programs are not dissimilar to moving files around on your own hard drive. You have two window-panes: one side is the files on your computer, the other side is the files on the remote computer – in between is an arrow and once you have selected the relevant files this arrow is clicked to copy the files from one side to the other.

*The information you will need to know*
Whether you use Microsoft Publisher's program or an alternative FTP is up to you. Either way you will need to know your ISP's address for the computer server it uses to store subscribers' home pages on, as this will be different from the ordinary log-on address. This is usually given in the **help files** of your ISP, or in any literature you may have been sent from them. Whichever form of uploading you choose, you will be prompted to enter this address, along with your user ID and password. Providing everything is correct, you will be logged on to your own personal web space and the program can then begin transferring your files.

### Viewing and advertising your page
Your site will be available for viewing immediately but nobody will be able to find it unless they know the address. Check out the search engines mentioned earlier and look for the link '**submit a URL**' to tell them about your site. This is known as registering your page with a search engine and will help others to find your site when they enter keywords as described earlier. The more engines you register with, the more chances of getting people to look at your site. You may not get listed as the number one, but at least people will have more of a chance to come across your site than if you do nothing.

You could look for other sites of similar content and put a hyperlink on your site to theirs. Then you could e-mail them and ask them to do the same on their site to yours. The net is very friendly in this way and a lot of fun can be had.

### Rounding off
Most people who use the net never get around to using their web site space. This is a shame because it is a lot of fun being able to advertise yourself and your interests in the world.

If you enjoy communicating with others on the net, then why not use your web site to put your photo and some details about your interests for your new-found friends to see. You can then update it with new information and save the trouble of e-mailing everyone.

This can be very useful for those with family and friends scattered all over the world – and cheap too!

### CASE STUDY

### David's family web is a real spinner
David is a retired policeman and has three sons living in Canada,

Australia and Hong Kong respectively. Although spread across the globe, the family love to keep in touch – especially now that David and his wife are grandparents. They all arrange to set up a family web page of their own.

Each family unit set up their own web site and informed the rest of the family of the relevant addresses to those sites. Hyperlinks were added to each site to 'join' them together. They then posted bits of news, photos and sound files that the children had created, on to the pages. This became great fun and enabled them to keep in more regular contact without the expense of ringing and writing to each other separately. It also helped eliminate the need to think about the difference in time when contacting each other.

As the sites will only be of interest to the family they do not need to register with search engines. They just need to ensure that they know the addresses of all the web sites.

**PRACTICAL EXERCISE**

This short exercise shows you how each search engine can vary in the web site information it provides, using the same description.

1. Log on to your Internet service provider.
2. Choose a search engine either by selecting its icon from your provider's home page, or by typing in their address in the address bar.
3. In the **Search** box, type **Greetings Cards** and press the **search button** to retrieve the top ten sites that match the request.
4. Make a note of the first ten sites that the search engine displays, then try another search engine and compare the results.

We tried this example with four different search engines:

- http://www.altavista.com
- http://www.lycos.co.uk
- http://www.ukplus.co.uk
- http://www.yahoo.co.uk

Each gave a different list of the first ten sites. We were looking for **Virtual Cards** – we eventually found it on the **Yahoo!** site. Virtual Cards is a very good web site that allows you to send a card to another friend on the Internet. When the card has been read, you are informed. Their address is: http://www.prismweb.com.

# 8

# Essential Program Utilities to Consider

## KEEPING YOUR FILES SECRET WITH SECURITY PROGRAMS

There will no doubt come a time in your computer experience that you will want to keep prying eyes from some of your documents. This may not be because of secrecy but simply to stop your children from messing around where they could cause irreparable damage to your hard work – or vice versa!

*But I could use Windows User Profiles*
Although Windows allows you to set up multiple users on your system, with a password required for each user, this is not really as secure as it seems. If someone who is not authorised to use the computer switches it on, they can merely press the escape key when the log-on screen is displayed. This will give them access to everything, and even allow them to log on as a new user and give themselves a password.

The user log-on should be thought of solely as a convenience that enables different, personalised desktops for each user of the system, not as security.

### How do security programs work?
Security of files, programs and data is achieved by adding encryption. An encrypted or coded file cannot be accessed by an unauthorised individual and cannot be copied or deleted. There are many third party security programs available and the one we have used is **For Your Eyes Only** from the Norton stable. Once installed the system is managed from the Control Centre as shown in Figure 87.

### Explaining the user status
On a stand-alone computer, i.e. one that is not networked to another, For Your Eyes Only will give two types of user, the **Primary** and the **Secondary**. The primary user will have access to all files and folders whether encrypted or not, along with access to the security program set-up. The reason for this is quite straightforward: somebody has to be

## Essential Program Utilities to Consider 121

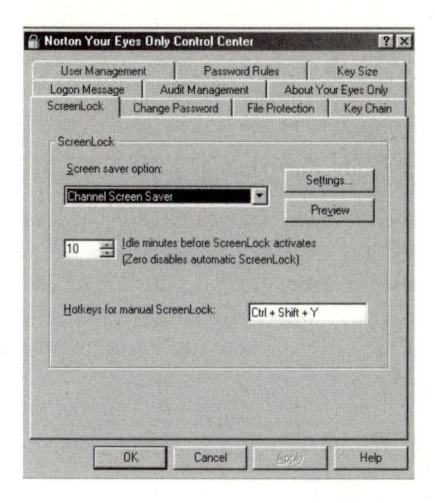

Fig. 87. Norton's Control Centre.

responsible for the system and they can't be denied access to anything on that system or they would have no effective control. There can only be one primary user on the system.

There can be as many secondary users on the system as you want. Each secondary user has their own password and can encrypt files that they wish other secondary users not to have access to. This is all done in the **Explorer** window. When For Your Eyes Only is installed it adds the encryption options to the right-click mouse menu. There are two principal encryption options available:

1. The first enables you to right-click on the file name and manually encrypt or decrypt it from the menu as shown in the first menu of Figure 88. Once this is done the icon next to the file will show a little

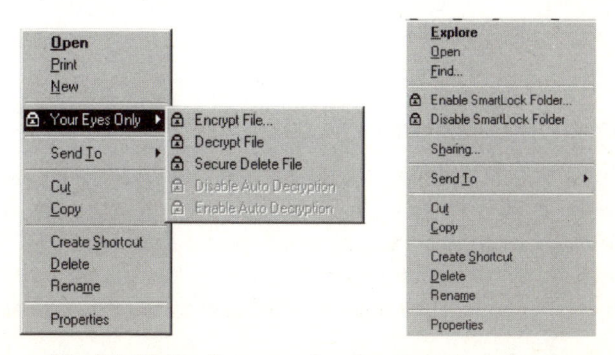

Fig. 88. Menus for manual and automatic encryption.

padlock. A manually encrypted file will not appear in the Open File dialogue box within a program. Before it can be accessed it has to be manually decrypted first.

2. The other option is to create a **Smartlock Folder** as seen in the other menu in Figure 88. Once created, the Smartlock Folder will automatically encrypt and decrypt files that are saved in it. Using this method, a different SmartLock Folder can be created for each user and will eliminate the possibility of forgetting to encrypt something and the hassle of having to go into Explorer and decrypt each file before you can use them.

### Restricting people from using a program

Programs can also be encrypted using the Smartlock method. This will prevent an unauthorised person from starting a program in the first place. A note of caution when using encryption programs, however: once a file has been encrypted, nobody can access it without a password – not even the person who created it. With a good encryption program there is no way around the problem of forgetting your password, no matter how important your work is.

### Using encrypted files on another computer

Other types of encryption software are available to make your files easier to transport. With the Norton program above, you must have it installed on each machine you wish to use your encrypted file on. This may not be convenient if you are transporting files on disk from one computer to another.

**PC Crypto** from McAfee solves this problem by encrypting the file with its password as a whole – you do not then need the program installed to open the file. To access the file on another machine you will just have to enter your password first. Once again, forget your password and you can forget your work!

### CREATING AND UNZIPPING COMPRESSED FILES

**File compression** is a technique used to enable data to take up less room when stored on disk. The actual mechanics of how this is done is quite complex and it is not necessary to understand it to use it, thank goodness. The process of compressing files is also widely known as **zipping** and this is a term that you will come across quite often, so it's handy to know what it's all about.

Many programs that you buy are compressed onto the CD or floppy disk and the install or set-up program that comes with them will uncompress them automatically for you. There are many different file compression types but the one that is most used, particularly on a home computer, is **WinZip**.

The WinZip program is available as shareware and is often found on magazine cover disks. If you are connected to the Internet you can download a copy of WinZip free from **http://www.winzip.com**. Using the program is fairly straightforward and we will run through an example of zipping and unzipping later in this section.

### So why would you bother zipping and unzipping files?

There are two main reasons for doing this. They both revolve around the precious resource of space. Not everybody will have massive hard drives and sometimes, when you are running short, the answer will be to zip up some of the stuff you want to keep but perhaps don't use very often.

- Text files can be reduced in size by as much as 90 per cent after compression, so if you keep copies of all the letters you send, then compressing them is a good idea. This action is sometimes known as **archiving**.

- Another reason for zipping is the old **floppy disk**. If you want to copy to floppy disk a file that is too big to fit on it, then WinZip will allow you to spread it over as many disks as it takes. When you want to put it onto another computer then WinZip will manage this for you and rebuild the files and directories. Pretty handy stuff!

So let's see WinZip in action. It is a good idea to create a new folder on your C: drive in which to store all your zip files. Do this now before starting WinZip.

### Using WinZip to compress selected files

The first thing to do is to start the program running by double-clicking on the desktop icon or selecting it from the menu. Click on the **I agree** button, if you decide to purchase the program you will not be bothered by this screen. If you choose to view it with the **Classic** style when installing you will see the initial screen as in Figure 89, only the viewing area will be blank until you open a zip file as we have done here. The file in Figure 89 shows all the documents inside one zip file that we will now create.

**124** Moving On from Computer Basics

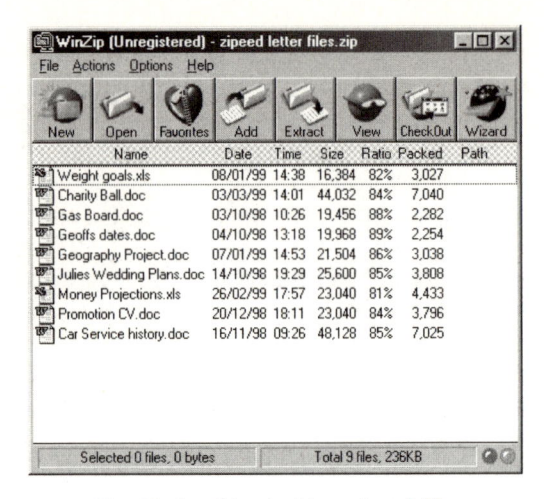

Fig. 89. Looking inside a zipped file.

1. To create a new zip file, click on the **New** button.
2. In the **New Archive** dialogue box, as shown in Figure 90, fill in the **File name** area with a suitable name for your zip file.
3. In the **Create** box, navigate your way to the location where you want to place your zipped file when it is created. Click OK.
4. Next, in the **Add** dialogue box, locate the files you wish to add to the zip file and highlight them as shown in Figure 91. You can select more than one file at a time by holding down the **Ctrl** key while you are selecting.

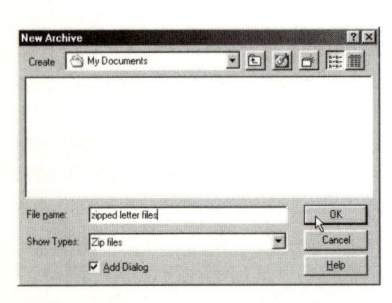

Fig. 90. Creating a zipped file.

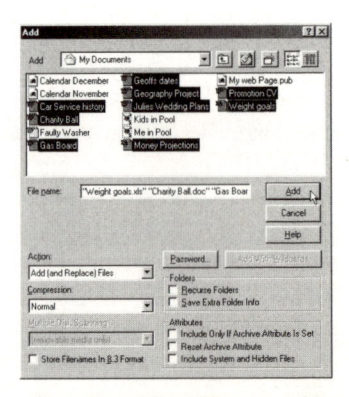

Fig. 91. Adding files to a zip.

5. Click on **Add** and all the highlighted individual files will become one zip file.

You can return to the Add box if you have files in other folders that you also wish to put into the zip file. Click on the **Add** icon at the top of the window to return and repeat the process of highlighting the relevant files.

*Does this process delete the original files?*
No. All the zip process does is to make a copy of all the chosen files and compress them into one large file. If the reason you are doing this is to conserve space, you will have to go back to your document folders and delete the original files – a copy of each is safe in the zip file.

### Viewing and extracting from a zipped file

Any zipped file can be viewed to see what files are inside it within WinZip. Click on the **Open** button and select the relevant zip file to display its contents. It will display as shown in Figure 89.

An individual file, or selection of files using the Ctrl key, can be highlighted for pulling out of the zip file using the **Extract** button. A dialogue box asking where you wish to extract the file to will be displayed. This box also gives you the option to extract just the selected files, or all files as seen on the left side of Figure 92.

Once the file or files are extracted, they can be used in the normal way from the folder you extracted them to. Extracting a file does not remove it from the zip file, it simply decompresses a copy of the one chosen.

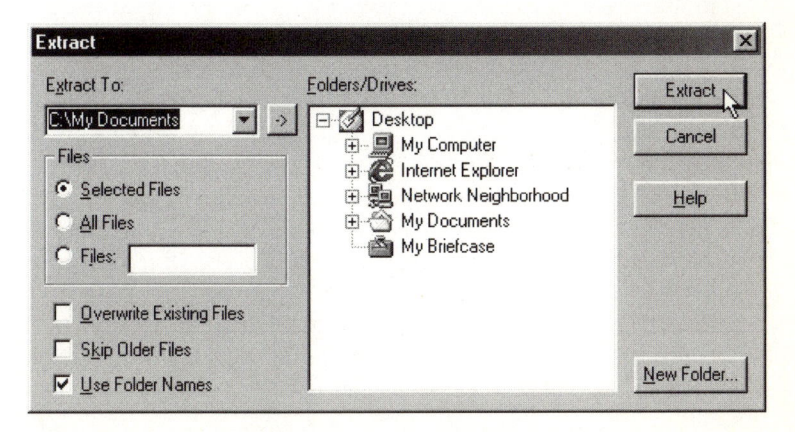

Fig. 92. Extracting from a zipped file.

## Spanning large zip files over multiple disks

You may have experienced trying to copy a large file onto a floppy disk. It may whirr about a bit and eventually finish but only to reveal there is nothing on the disk – it hasn't copied anything. Your computer hasn't thrown a wobbly, it will have attempted to copy the file, but when it realised that the file was bigger than the available space on a floppy disk, it aborted the operation because it is not able to do that without a special program. Windows 98 is a little cleverer than that – it shows you a message as in Figure 93.

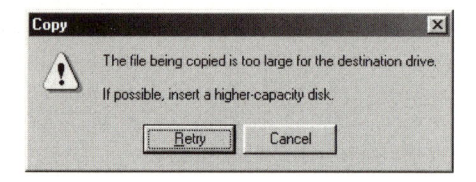

Fig. 93. A Windows warning.

**Disk spanning** is the name given to a file or number of files that are zipped to floppy disks and that take up more space than one disk will hold. Once the first disk is full you will be asked to insert subsequent disks until the file has been transferred. Make sure that you have enough formatted floppies to hand before starting the process.

The method used is the same as for a normal zipping procedure as described earlier but select the A: drive as the destination for the saved file. In other words, you have to create the zip file on the floppy disk first in the **New Archive** dialogue box, and then add the files to it. It is important to label the disks with the order in which they were inserted because the final disk will contain the index of files stored. You will not be able to see this index file but WinZip will need to read it before it can rebuild the files contained on it.

## Extracting the collection of large files

When decompressing a spanned file you will be asked to insert the last disk first, so that WinZip can read the index. You will then have to remove it and put in the disk containing the file you wish to extract. Don't worry about this, you won't know what disk is required but WinZip will and will ask you for the relevant number. This is why it is so important to label them correctly. As in the previous example, you will have to select a directory for the files to be decompressed into and once again click on **extract**. If the selected file spans more than one disk, you will be prompted for each one that is required.

The whole process of zipping and unzipping probably sounds a little cumbersome but once you have done it a couple of times you will realise how easy it is and how useful.

## THE ADVANTAGES OF CD WRITERS AND ZIP DRIVES

### Remembering the floppy disk
Backing up large amounts of data has in the past been a bit of a problem. However, the computer industry has responded in a number of ways. In years gone by, the floppy disk was the only option for most of us, and it still has its place and its uses:

- in an emergency for booting your computer
- quick transfer of smaller files for safe keeping or putting on another machine
- they are cheap
- easy to store and fit neatly into your pocket.

However, they are not so useful with larger files.

### Tape streaming as an alternative
An alternative to the floppy disk is the tape drive. Although these devices have been around for a long time in commercial circles, their large size and expense saw few homes with one. Tape drives have been available to the home user for a few years now and can be fitted internally in a free drive bay. They use tapes similar to those used by some video cameras and are small enough to fit easily into your pocket.

The drawback with any form of tape drive is speed. If you perform regular backups of large amounts of data you will be spending a considerable amount of time just waiting. If you do use a tape drive then set it up to perform the backup when you go to lunch or have finished for the day.

### The convenience of a Zip drive
Another popular alternative is the Zip drive. This again will fit inside your computer and takes a form of floppy disk. These disks, however, hold much more information than a conventional floppy disk – in fact about the same amount as 70 conventional floppies. They are also available as superdisks that can hold up to 200 Mb of information. These drives are also very much quicker than the conventional floppy, up to 20 times faster.

Other drives are also available in larger capacities, but most home and small business users wouldn't justify the expense involved unless there was a genuine need, e.g. large amounts of video editing.

### The benefits of a CD writer and re-writer

Perhaps the most useful mass storage medium available to the home user, other than the hard drive of course, is the **CD writer**. Writable CDs are now very cheap to buy and can hold around 650 Mb of data. These drives can read conventional CDs as well as writing them so they can replace your normal CD and save you some space. With the correct software, copyright permitting of course, you can make copies of CDs you already have, both music and data.

CD writers are also very useful for backing up large amounts of archived data (data you want to keep but do not have to change, like copies of letters sent) or for saving a backup of your hard disk ready for that dreaded format. CDs are also a very safe medium to store data on. Both floppy disks and tapes are prone to shock, magnetic forces, temperature, and poor handling, all of which can corrupt the data stored on them. CDs, on the other hand, are extremely durable and easy to store.

If you decide to invest in a CD writer, then opt for one that can handle re-writable disks. The original CDs (Gold Disks) could only be written to once, which meant that if you only put a small file on it then you could not add to it later. This wasted disk space and increased the number you had to store. With the re-writable CDs you can keep adding things until you have a full disk, saving time, storage and money. CDs are also a convenient medium for moving large amounts of data from one computer to another, as most computers will have a CD-ROM drive fitted.

### In summary

Data backup is an area that most computer users are very sloppy about. If you have important data stored on your computer, make sure it is backed up, preferably on some sort of removable medium. If your hard drive fails, they are cheap enough to replace, but don't forget that anything stored on the old one will be lost for good.

We deal with many people who are bemoaning their lot because we can't retrieve lost data from a failed disk. One firm lost two years' worth of business accounts because of a failed hard drive. If they had performed regular backups to CD or removable disk, this would not have happened.

## CREATING PARTITIONS AND DISK IMAGING

### A little history explained on partitioning

Partitioning hard disks used to be far more necessary in the earlier days of computing than it is now. The main reason for this was that most DOS operating systems prior to Windows 95 could not recognise a hard disk bigger that 512 Mb. This meant that if you had a hard disk of one gigabyte it would have to be partitioned, or divided, into two or more drives no bigger than 512 Mb in order to make full use of it. DOS 6 and the earlier versions of Windows 95 improved on this to allow hard disks of up to 2Gb to be seen as a single drive. Later versions of Windows 95 and Windows 98 offered greater improvements by using FAT 32, enabling drives with much larger capacities to be viewed as a single drive.

Hard disk sizes have continued to grow and it is not uncommon to see computers with 14 Gb or more. Such drives do not now have to be partitioned in order to access all their space.

### Addressing partitions

Each partition is seen by the operating system as a separate drive and is assigned a drive letter. If you had a drive partitioned into three they would be assigned the letters C:, D: and E: as in Figure 94. The computer in Figure 94 also has a removable drive F: which is the **Camera Connect** as described in Chapter 2. The CD-ROM therefore has the letter G:. As you can see, it could become a bit confusing trying to remember just where you saved that file or where you installed that particular program.

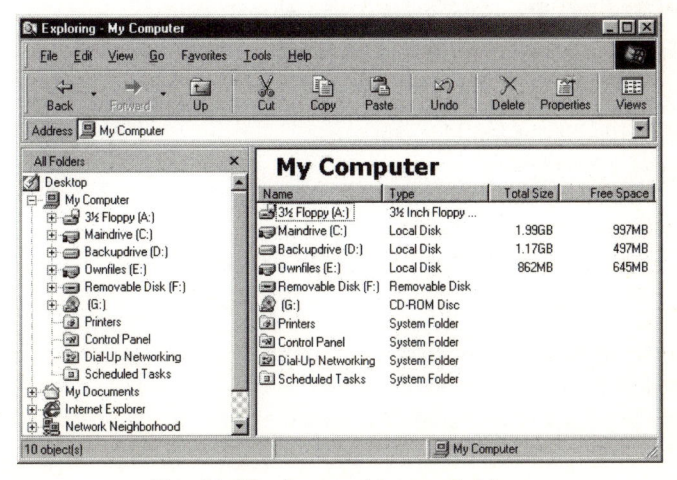

Fig. 94. Viewing partitions and drives.

### The advantages of partitioning

Partitioning a larger drive does have its advantages. When you open a file the computer has first to find it and then to read it. If files have become fragmented, then the bigger the drive the longer this process will take, so smaller drives can make reads and writes a lot quicker.

The main advantage of having at least one partition other than the C: drive is **security**. If, for some reason (and there are hundreds of possible ones), your system throws a wobbly and you have to reformat your C: drive, you could lose vital data stored on it. We have already seen that some files are not convenient to back up easily onto floppy, so if all work is saved to the second (D:) partition, it would be kept safe in case the C: drive should have to be reformatted. We will look at another benefit when we discuss disk imaging later in this section.

### How do you go about creating a partition on your disk?

There are two options available to you.

*Using the DOS utility FDISK*

This comes on your operating system disk and should only be used if you are starting from scratch with a blank hard drive. If you aren't starting from scratch yet, and you use this utility, you soon will be, as it destroys all data on the hard drive. For this reason you should make sure that you are well prepared:

- Have available a **bootable floppy disk** containing an **autoexec.bat** and **config.sys** that will set up your CD drivers, along with copies of the files **fdisk.com**, **format.com** and **mscdex.exe**.

- Have your operating system CD-ROM disks to hand.

- Make sure all your work is saved to a removable medium, i.e. floppy disk, zip disk or another computer.

- Have you got all the program disks you will need to re-install?

- Make sure you have your operating system manuals to hand or some other reference material that explains the use of FDISK fully.

**Warning**: FDISK is a DOS utility and should not be used without all the steps listed above being taken. The use of this command will make your hard drive unusable until the procedure has been carried out properly.

*Using third party utilities*

The easiest way to create partitions is to use a third-party utility such as **Partition Magic**. This will enable you to create, delete and alter the size of partitions 'on the fly'. This saves all the hassle of having to start again with reformatting and reloading all your programs and valuable data, but it is still a good idea to back up important files before you start just to be on the safe side.

Although Partition Magic runs in DOS it can be run from Windows 95/98 and has a Windows 95/98 look, to make you feel at home. When you have finished, it will restart Windows automatically. If you are at all unsure about using the FDISK utility mentioned previously, then it is recommended that you adopt this method.

## Gaining valuable time from disk imaging

This is the ultimate in reasons for having at least one partition on your disk. Disk imaging software is not expensive – especially when compared to the amount of work it will save you in the future. If you have ever had to reformat your drive you will know just how long it takes to get it set up again just the way you want it. You will probably have to spend a whole day loading and setting up programs, configuring your games, and setting all the preferences. If this is you then you will appreciate how nice it would be to be able to accomplish the whole job in as little as ten minutes!

A **disk image** is a backup of one entire partition of the hard drive – complete with all programs, files and configuration settings. If you then have a disaster on a partition – for example, your C: drive – this can be restored using the imaging package.

Disasters can happen at any time:

- A demo disk may cause confusing errors to appear.
- System files may accidentally get deleted.
- A virus may get onto your hard drive.
- A lot of rubbish may have been installed by your children.

The initial image can be made to another partition for the quickest restoration, such as the D: drive. A removable medium such as a Zip drive or CD writer can also be used if your hard drive is too small to partition, provided its storage capacity is sufficient.

*When is the best time to do an image?*
An image can be taken at any time, but the trick with this one is to start from scratch.

1. Partition and format your hard drive accordingly.

2. Do a clean installation of Windows on your C: drive, set up how you like it.

3. Ensure all your peripherals are correctly configured – printer, modem, etc.

4. Load on the programs you use regularly and set them up to your requirements.

5. Defragment your C: drive so that all files are neatly placed.

6. Load the imaging software onto another partition, such as the D: drive

7. Run the program and image your C: drive to it.

As this utility makes a copy of an entire partition it cannot be created on or restored from the same partition it is imaging, hence the need for the second partition or Zip drive. Once this image has been created, if a disaster happens with your C: drive, then simply restore your original set-up from the image.

### Computer manufacturer images

When computer manufacturers build machines they use a drive image program to install all the software that comes pre-installed on it. Most manufacturers also copy an image of the drive onto a CD that will come with the machine usually labelled something like 'Emergency Start-up Disk'. Once inserted you will be able to restore the computer to its original factory settings. However, it will not include programs you have added since or any work you have saved.

### CASE STUDY

#### Sarah and Kevin tighten their home security

Sarah and Kevin run a small business from home. They have purchased their first computer, a top-of-the-range model that they hope will fulfil their needs for some time to come. They have two children, aged seven and twelve, who will also want to benefit from the system.

Sarah, who will be using the computer the most, decides to purchase an encryption package to provide some security and control over the programs installed. She will organise each member of the family with a password. This password will determine the programs that each member can access. This will ensure that everyone can have their privacy (and hopefully avoid arguments) and that Sarah will still maintain control and security of the business data and personal information should the system ever be stolen.

# 9

# Making Use of Communication Resources

You may, for one reason or another, end up running more than one computer. This could be because you have upgraded by buying a new machine and decide to keep the old one for your children. Another more obvious reason would be because you need to use a laptop whilst out and about, but keep a desktop at home for the convenience of the full-size screen and keyboard.

Whatever the reason, you will probably want to be able to link the two machines together at some point. We will now discuss the methods that make this possible.

- **Direct Cable Connection** is a useful way of linking two computers that are physically close to each other by using a cable that is plugged into a port on the back of each computer, as and when required. This is most often the more convenient choice with portable-to-desktop connections. This subject is covered in Chapter 1.

- **Networking** two desktops together within the same vicinity gives you more freedom along with the added benefit of each computer being able to use the other's resources. The advantage of this over Direct Cable Connection is that it is faster and a more permanent connection that can be activated at any time from the desktop.

- When connecting two computers that are in different locations, such as your home computer with a laptop while on the road, the use of a **modem** in each machine is needed, along with special software that allows the connection to be active.

## NETWORKING TWO COMPUTERS TOGETHER

There are various types of network connections available – most are intended for the office environment and can be extremely complex involving dozens of computers. Such networks require a lot of experience and skilled people to install and operate them. The type of connection that we will cover is simple and ideally suited to the home or small business environment.

It involves having two independent computers – each with their own hard drive that has an operating system such as Windows installed. Each computer should also have their own programs loaded. A simple network card is installed into a spare slot inside each computer and a special connector is attached to the cards that enable a length of network cable to link the two together. Each computer then has the ability, subject to correct configuration, to:

- share each other's files
- use the same printer
- copy items from one to the other
- play a network game
- use the other's CD-ROM and floppy disk drive
- use the same modem (this requires extra software and specific circumstances).

### Configurations needed for each computer

To enable the computers to understand each other, they both have to have the same workgroup name, the same protocols installed and be using the same client for network logging on. In addition, each computer has to be given an individual name and has to enable sharing conditions. Don't worry if all this sounds like complicated gobbledegook, it is quite straightforward and will be explained along the way.

In our example below, both computers are running Windows 98 – although it would be exactly the same if one were using Windows 95. We have installed two **PCI NE2000 compatible plug-and-play network cards**, one in each machine. The T connectors and terminators that came with the cards have been fitted onto a 10-metre length of network cable and plugged into the card.

### Explaining a little technical knowledge

The posh name for cabling up a network is **topology** and there are several different types – ours will be a bus topology, which is the simplest form of cabling. **Ethernet** is a term meaning a standard that is adopted for network specifications and components used. One of the implementations of these standards is called **Thinnet** – sometimes referred to as **10Base2**.

This is the one we shall use – it consists of a network cable segment with terminators at each end. The cable is a special coaxial cable similar to that of a TV aerial. A terminator is required at each end of the network cable, so no matter how many computers are connected you still only use two terminators. The plugs used to connect it all are **BNC connectors** on the adapter card and **T connectors** on the cable.

Thinnet is one of the least expensive methods of implementing an Ethernet network. **Fast Ethernet**, also called **100BaseX**, is an extension of the Ethernet standard that operates at a speed of 100 Mbps – ten times faster than the 10Base2.

On the software side, **protocol** is a word you may come across quite often. **Protocol** in computer terms means a set of rules that define how communications are to take place in a network. It follows that both computers must be pursuing the same rules – this is known as **handshaking**.

### Setting up the machines

Let us begin by loading the drivers and configuring each machine. You may need your Windows disk inserted in the CD-ROM.

1. Click the **Add New Hardware** button in the Control Panel and allow the wizard to search for your new adapter card. The wizard will load and configure the 32-bit protected mode NDIS 5 driver.

2. In **Control Panel** again, select the **Network** icon. This shows a dialogue box similar to that shown in Figure 95. Ensure that both

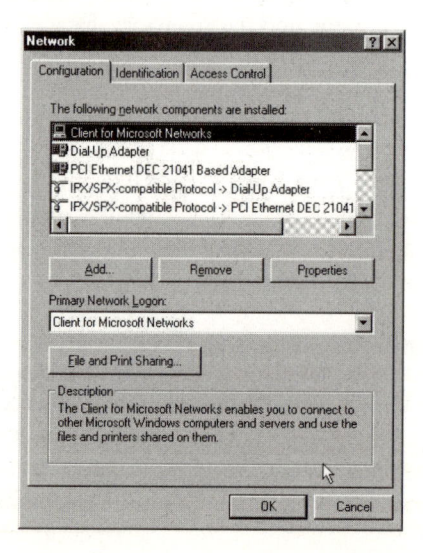

Fig. 95. The network configuration box.

computers use the same Primary Network Log-on – Client for Microsoft Networks is suitable in most cases. If it is not there, click **Add**, select **Client** and click **Add** again.

3. Check which **protocols** are already installed, if any – these can be found in the area at the top. The three most common protocols are **TCP/IP, NetBEUI** and **IPX/SPX**. If you are unsure which one you need to run this network, install all three, it won't do any harm. There may already be at least one installed if you are connected to the Internet. To install further ones, click the **Add** button, choose **Protocol**, then from the **Microsoft Manufacturer** click on the required ones in turn.

4. Next, click on the **File** and **Print Sharing** tab. Ensure the top box is checked, as seen in Figure 96, so that the other computer can view this one. If the computer has a printer attached that you will want to access with the other computer, check the bottom box.

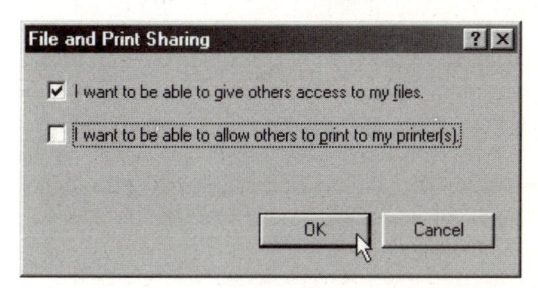

Fig. 96. Allowing file and print sharing.

5. Now go to the **Identification** tab and give your computer an individual name. In the **Workgroup** space, ensure both computers have the same workgroup name. The **Computer Description** is optional.

6. Click OK and when your computer has finished loading any files needed following your selections, you will more than likely have to restart it for the new settings to take effect.

7. You now need to decide which drives, files and peripherals you are going to share. To share the whole of any particular drive, double click **My Computer**, right-click the drive icon and select **Sharing** from the menu – check the **Shared As** box and give the drive an identification name. If you only want to share particular folders, then

double-click on the drive where the folders are located and right-click each one required, naming them as described above. Next, check one of the access boxes – **Depends on Password** option provides a little bit of safety when connected to the Internet. If you happen to be using the same protocol as a hacker, it may be possible for them to access your hard drive too, but not if he doesn't know your password!

8. Go through the same process for each drive, folder or printer that you wish to share with the other computer. This can be done in either **My Computer** or **Explorer**. Restart both computers and you are networked.

## CONNECTING TO ANOTHER LOCAL COMPUTER

Connecting to another computer can be done in many ways. In this section we will see how it is done via a network with **Network Neighbourhood** and by **mapping** a drive. Later we will discuss what is needed for connecting to a distant computer via a modem.

Double-click the **Network Neighbourhood** icon on the desktop of one of the computers. Provided that they are turned on, you will see the name of the workgroup and any computer connected to the network. By selecting **Views** as shown in Figure 97 you can change the appearance so that it matches the way you are used to navigating through Windows Explorer on your own computer.

By double-clicking on one of the icons, you will be able to access any folders or drives that have been configured for sharing with another computer. You will not be able to see or access any that are not shared. If for

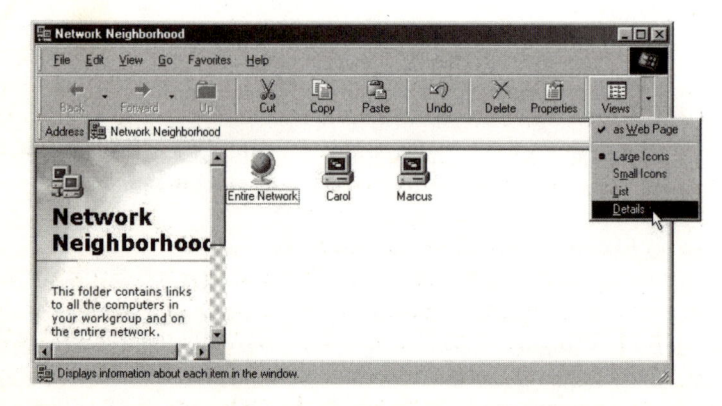

Fig. 97. The Network Neighbourhood screen.

any reason you cannot see something that you expected to be able to access, re-check the sharing properties on the other computer.

### Mapping a network drive

You can also access another computer's shared resources by assigning a drive letter on your own computer and directing the path accordingly. This is known as **mapping a drive**. One way of doing this is in Windows Explorer as follows:

- From the **Tools** menu select **Map Network Drive**.
- Windows will automatically assign the next available drive letter that's available.
- Enter the path command which must start with two backslashes, followed by the computer name, then another backslash followed by the shared resources name as shown in Figure 98.
- Click OK and this shared resource will now be available as if it was an additional hard drive on your own computer.

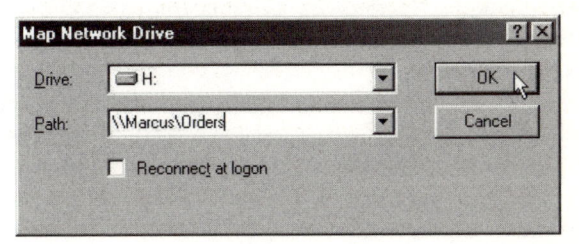

Fig. 98. Mapping a drive.

If an error message is shown, such as 'The share name was not found, be sure you typed it correctly' or 'This device does not exist on the network', check that the computer you are trying to connect to has shared this resource and that you are typing its shared name correctly. The folder name on the computer is not necessarily its shared name.

### Having fun with networked computers

There are many games available that allow you to play via a network. This means playing against others on **your** network and has nothing to do with the Internet. When you are networked, a game such as **Duke Nukem** or **Quake** allows you to play as you would in the normal game, but both of you (or more) appear within the same game.

You can see each other, shoot each other or play co-operatively against the baddies, conquering the challenge together. Hours of fun can be had playing like this. The only downside is that the game will normally only run at the speed of the slowest machine, and there is often no facility to save a game when playing in this mode.

## LINKING TO REMOTE COMPUTERS

It is the norm now for business people to be on the road with their laptop computers and mobile phones. People from all walks of life go home early and log on to their office computer to finish off work in a quieter environment. How is it all possible and what is involved?

### Using Windows Dial Up Networking (DUN)

Included with both Windows 95 and Windows 98 is a facility called Dial Up Networking (DUN). It may not be installed by default but can be added from the Windows Set Up tab in the Add/Remove Programs.

As its name suggests, it allows one computer – laptop or desktop – to connect with another via the telephone line. Both computers have to be fitted with a modem and have DUN loaded and running to allow connections to be made.

Setting up Dial Up Networking is fairly straightforward and is ideal for transferring files and data when you are away from your base computer. Providing all the sharing of files and setting of network protocols has been carried out as described earlier, the following method is used to set a computer as a remote host:

- Ensure **Dial Up Networking** *and* **Dial Up Server** are installed – if not, select them from **Control Panel/Add-Remove Programs/Windows Setup/Communications**.
- Click on **Start/Programs/Accessories/Communications/Dial Up Networking**.
- From the **Connections** menu, select **Dial Up Server**.
- Check the box **Allow Caller Access** as seen in Figure 99 and click **Apply**.
- The computer is now ready to receive an incoming call from another computer.

The main snag with this type of connection is the need to know in

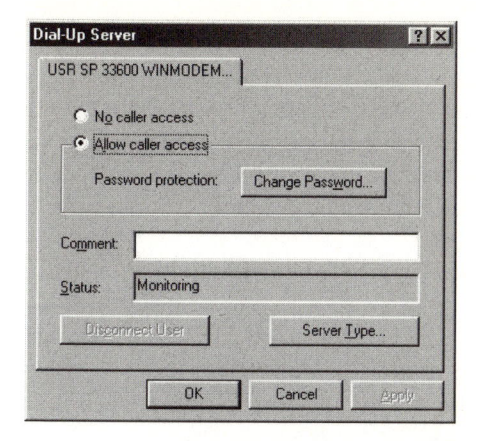

Fig. 99. Windows remote Dial Up Networking.

advance that you are going to use it. The host computer has to be expecting your call. This is not a problem if you can ring your home or office and there is somebody to set it up for you when required. If you just leave it set up permanently, you will be unable to use the phone line for anything else incoming, as the computer will answer all calls on the assumption it is another computer calling.

DUN can also be painfully slow at moving data around, taking as long as twenty minutes or so to move a megabyte of data. Once connected, your remote computer is treated just as another computer on the network. Provided file and print sharing are activated, you can print documents from your laptop using your printer at home, so that they will be ready to read when you get there.

Your security options are also limited. Once connected, anyone can access any computer on the network with potentially disastrous results. In short, it's nice to have available in an emergency, but not ideally suited if you have to use remote access regularly.

### Connection requirements the easy way

The use of additional software installed and running can make connection quick and easy. Programs such as Norton's **PC Anywhere** allow quick configuration and good security measures so that you are unlikely to have any unwanted guests viewing your computer's content.

Requirements that we have already discussed such as file sharing, computer naming and the same networking protocols have to be adhered to as well as both computers having a modem.

## Setting up the host

The host is the computer you will connect to. We will use an example where Tony runs his own business. At the weekend his wife likes him to be at home – even if he still needs to do some work, at least she has his company and can involve herself in what he is achieving within the business while keeping her eye on the children.

*It's Friday afternoon and Tony sets the business computer up as a host*

1. He starts PC Anywhere running by double-clicking on the icon. He now selects the button to **Be A Host PC**. He has the options of setting it up through a direct connection, a modem or a network, as seen in Figure 100. He will use the modem connection but wants to ensure that nobody else can dial into the computer.

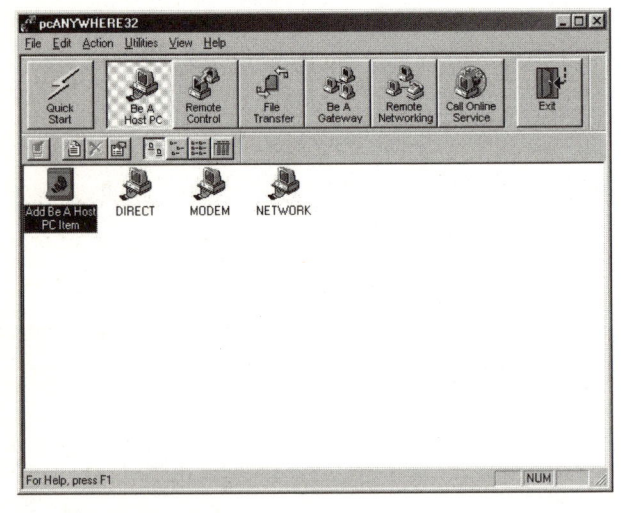

Fig. 100. Norton PC Anywhere dial-up networking.

2. By right-clicking on the **modem** icon and selecting **properties** he can implement security options. On the **Settings** tab he can put in a **Log-in** name and password that only he knows. This will mean that when he calls the office computer from home, he will first have to enter these details before the computer will allow him to do anything.

3. On the **Callback** tab, shown in Figure 101, he ticks for the office computer to call him back. This serves two purposes for Tony. Firstly, the phone call charges will go on his business telephone bill rather than

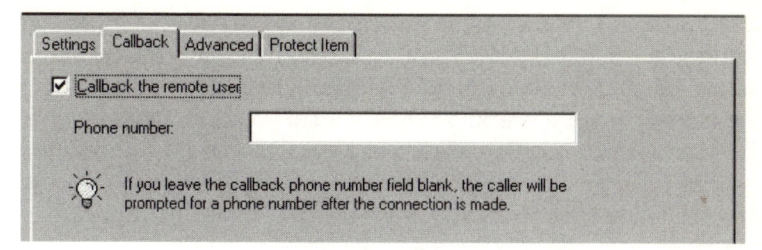

Fig. 101. Security options are strongly advised.

his home. Secondly, the telephone number entered is the only number the computer will communicate with, thus preventing unwanted persons from connecting with his computer over the weekend.

4. He checks the **Advanced** tab and ensures that the **Superuser** selection has been ticked. By doing this, Tony will have full access to the firm's computer. If at a later date he allows other members of his staff to connect to the computer remotely, he can limit their access in this section. This way he can control its use and restrict others, perhaps, to downloading work files to the computer but nothing else.

5. Tony clicks OK and is now ready to set the computer to its waiting state – this means it is ready to receive an incoming call. This is done simply by double-clicking on the **modem** icon. He can now leave the office, turning off the screen if he wishes, so that any onlookers do not realise the computer is still on.

## Calling from the remote location

Over the weekend when Tony wants to carry out some work, he achieves this in the following way:

- He runs the PC Anywhere program on his home computer.
- He clicks on the **Remote Control** button – this is used for connection to a host.
- A dialogue box prompts him to enter the phone number to dial.
- Once connected, he enters his log-in name and password.
- The host computer displays a message that he will be called back.
- One minute later, the phone rings and the two computers become connected.

What Tony will see is a window on his desktop that is in fact the desktop of the host computer. He can then use his mouse to navigate around the office computer as if he was there in person. Programs can be run and files copied and pasted from one machine to another as if the host computer was just another hard drive on his home computer.

Anyone at the other end of a connection such as this would see the mouse moving around on the desktop as if somebody was there doing it – a bit spooky really but fascinating and useful.

## CASE STUDY

### Sue installs a simple network

Sue runs a dating agency and, like many businesses, has kept clients' details on computer for some time. Lately business has been very brisk and she has taken on a secretary to perform routine office chores, including the entering of customer details into the database.

It soon becomes apparent that Sue often needs access to the computer at the same time as her secretary, so she decides to buy another system. As she needs to have the up-to-date information at her fingertips, Sue networks the two computers together. This brings her the added benefit of being able to perform a nightly backup from one machine to the other. In the event of one machine breaking down, only a very small amount of information will be lost.

# 10
## When Things Start to Go Wrong

To solve computer problems successfully, it is necessary to think logically. Many times a computer will do something unexpected and we wonder why. Most times this will be because we haven't asked it to perform a task in the right way. We are used to communicating with other humans and in that interaction many things can be left unsaid – because we understand the meaning that goes with the words. For some reason we assume the computer can do the same.

Computers are not intelligent and so take everything quite literally and at face value. They take their instructions from the programs that run them, and you, in turn, activate those instructions from your keyboard or mouse. If the instructions are wrong, the result will be wrong. If a program has not been loaded or configured properly or if files have become corrupted, the computer won't know, or care. It will simply carry on trying to follow instructions as best it can and leave you to worry about whether the end result is right or not.

We expect computers to be right all the time, but sadly this is not always the case. Just like any other appliance we have in the home, they need maintenance and care. Luckily most of this can be accomplished by the user with the help of programs such as **Defrag** and **Scandisk** and by taking some simple precautions when loading or removing programs.

In this section we will try to give you some pointers to correcting some of the more common wobblies your system may throw.

**SAVING YOURSELF SOME FRUSTRATION**

Computers can be very frustrating when they do go wrong because there may possibly be only one minor thing amiss, but finding it can take hours of elimination processing. The fault may be temporary or permanent, it may be down to one particular program, a failing chip inside the machine, or hardware conflicts. There are certain actions that can be followed to avoid calling an engineer initially and it is these that we will discuss. It does not cover all eventualities by any means, but if it only prevents one call-out, hopefully it will have been worth the cost of this book.

Get into the good habit of regularly saving your work. Clicking on the floppy disk icon to save something takes only a second. If saving is done every fifteen minutes or so then this is the maximum amount of time it will take you to get back to where you were if anything goes wrong. The need for saving and backing up your work cannot be over-stressed.

When an error occurs, it will often lock up your system, preventing you from saving a file that you are in the middle of creating. If the file was saved a few minutes before the error occurs, that copy will more than likely still be safe. This then allows you to restart the computer, hopefully clearing the error and returning to your previously saved copy of work with the smallest amount of disruption.

## DIAGNOSING WHERE THE BLAME LIES

When an error occurs, always ask yourself the following questions to assist in diagnosing the problem:

### Have I just turned the computer on?

Errors do not always become apparent until the computer has been switched off and then restarted. This is especially so for accidentally deleted files – it is not until the file is needed that the error occurs. For example, Windows loads many reference files on boot up, so when you ask it to do something, it knows where to go and what to do. If you remove one of those files – it may not affect it straight away because:

- either the instructions from the file are already loaded in memory
- or you are not requesting the relevant program to which it is attached.

However, on the next boot up it will be saying 'where's so and so ... I know I had it last time but it isn't here now, what shall I do?' and the error occurs.

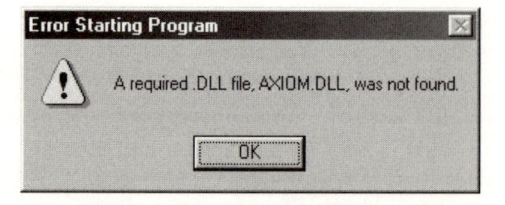

Fig. 102. Common error missing file box.

Figure 102 shows a typical error when starting a program that has had an important .DLL file accidentally deleted. If it is not available in the recycle bin to restore, the only option is to reload the program so that the missing file can be replaced. One of the commonest causes of such errors happens when uninstalling programs. If you say *Yes* to removing a shared file, it may just be that you deleted a file necessary for one of your other programs to run.

### Have I recently loaded a new program?
If the computer was behaving properly before the program was loaded, but is now throwing errors up on the screen, the new program could be conflicting with other programs or your machine. Try uninstalling the program and carry out a hard reboot of the system to see if the computer settles down again.

### Is it the first time using a particular program?
If a program isn't behaving the way you think it should, it may be that it is not loaded into the computer properly, or that it has a few configuration settings that need adjusting. If the problems are only happening while you are working within a particular program, then it is more than likely the program or its individual settings that are at fault.

### Does the error occur in similar programs?
If a similar problem happens in more than one program, then the cause may be directed at either the operating system or the computer itself. For example, if the sound worked fine on one of the loaded games but not on another, that would point to the offending program being at fault. If the sound didn't work on any programs, it would point to the sound card or its drivers being the problem.

### What was I doing prior to the error occurring?
It could be something you did within the program that triggered a bug. There can still be bugs in programs when they are sold to the public – they might only be triggered if you are using certain hardware or software. Checking with the technical support lines can highlight these. It is also worth viewing the **Read Me** files that come with the program. These sometimes contain known faults that were discovered after the manual was printed and will indicate how they may be overcome.

## COMMON PROBLEMS YOU MAY COME ACROSS

There are many, but the usual ones that seem to crop up on most people's computer at some time or another are **general protection faults**, **illegal functions** and **fatal exceptions**. They all sound a lot worse than they usually turn out to be.

### Helping the engineer

When these errors do occur, they normally give some details about which program or file caused it. If you do end up calling an engineer to solve your problems, it will reduce diagnosis time, and therefore your cost, if you have as many details as possible about the problems. As soon as a fault occurs, write it down – keep a log of all errors – they may be connected. Figure 103 shows an 'illegal operation' – the details tab was clicked to reveal potentially important information for an engineer. The following other information will be useful to an engineer:

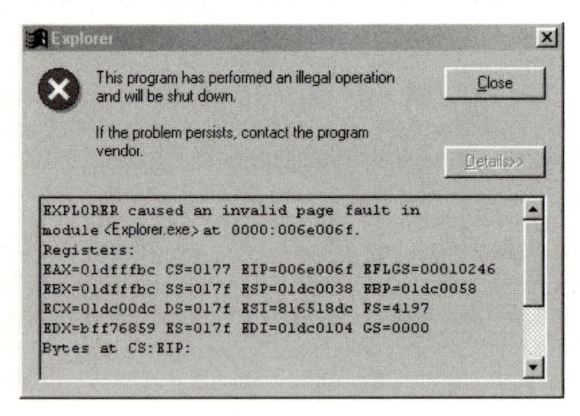

Fig. 103. Illegal operation error box.

- **date** the error happened – this will show if it is a regular occurrence
- **type** of error – illegal operation, general protection, fatal exception, etc.
- **details** of the error – write down the full description
- what **program** you were using at the time
- what **action** you had to take, i.e. closing the program, rebooting, etc.
- whether it **solved** the problem at the time
- **any other events** – power failures, lights flickering, next door's house blew up!

## Ignoring the illegal operation

These errors can seem to happen for no reason at all – although it is obvious something caused it. It normally happens just as you click on something such as an icon that performs a specific task, and that is more than likely where the error is. Whatever task you asked the computer to do, it got confused and tried to do something it shouldn't.

The message may give you the opportunity to look at details of the illegal operation – you probably won't understand it, but take a note of which file caused it. You may also be given the opportunity to click on either **Close** or **Ignore**. Ignoring it very rarely works – the message will probably just pop up again a fraction of a second later. Closing it will shut down the program that caused the fault, losing any work you were processing. You may then be able to restart the program and carry on without problem – if not, a hard reboot of the computer is the next thing to try.

## Fatal exception and general protection faults

When these occur, it is normally something that is a little more serious. More often than not, your computer has become unstable and is not in a position to carry on with anything. You will probably have no option but to turn off your computer – wait at least ten seconds for all the static to die down inside, then try starting it again to see if the problem has cleared.

If you were not able to shut it down in the usual way – you simply had to turn it off – the Scandisk program will tell you that Windows was not shut down properly and it now needs to perform some routine checks. Let it go through these – it shouldn't take too long and if it does find any problems, it gives you a chance to correct them by telling scandisk to **Fix It**.

## Coping with frozen screens

Sometimes an error message may not appear at all. Everything just decides to stop working – your mouse or keyboard will not respond. This is normally down to some sort of conflict within programs or hardware on your computer, which can only be resolved by process of elimination. Check out the common diagnosing tips at the beginning of this chapter.

If your mouse appears frozen but your keyboard still responds, you could try using the Ctrl/Alt/Delete method to see if it highlights which program is at fault. Having the words 'Not responding' next to a program name is a good clue.

1. Hold down the **Ctrl** key and the **Alt** key with one hand.
2. Press the **Delete** key with the other.

3. If a program is showing as not responding, select it using the arrow keys.

4. Press the **Alt** key and the **E** on your keyboard to 'end the task'.

5. A second box may appear asking you to 'end the task' again.

If this doesn't unfreeze your screen, shut down the computer by pressing Ctrl/Alt/Delete again but this time press the **Alt** key with the **S** key to shut down the computer. Switch it off, wait ten seconds and restart it.

## RESOLVING PROBLEMS

The only way to resolve some problems will be to reboot your computer. Although this will not cure any serious problems, it may resolve minor glitches caused by things such as power fluctuations. If the faults reoccur often, you can attempt to resolve them in various ways before calling out the engineer.

Most of us have been told 'Never turn off your computer without closing it down properly.' This is true, but sometimes it is unavoidable and it will not harm the machine in any way. The worst that can happen is that you lose unsaved work.

### Remember:
Most on-site warranty agreements only cover the cost of the call-out if the problem is a physical fault with the hardware. If the problem turns out to be a software fault, you may have to foot the bill yourself.

### Understanding hard and soft reboots
A **soft reboot** means restarting your machine without actually switching off the power. This is also known as a **warm reboot**. It can be done in one of three ways:

- Press the **reset button** on the front of the computer.
- Choose **Restart** from the shut down menu as seen in Figure 104.
- Press the **Ctrl** key, **Alt** key and **Delete** key on your keyboard all at the same time.

Doing this allows Windows to initialise its start up files again – often used when you have loaded a new driver. Restarting in this way does not always clear the RAM memory of any information, so if you have a

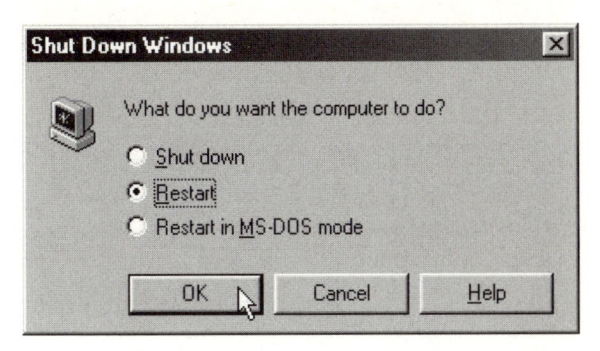

Fig. 104. Restarting the computer.

problem that may exist in RAM memory it is best to do a hard reboot.

*Clearing the memory with a hard reboot*
A **hard reboot** is when you turn off the machine at the power switch. This allows all the components inside the machine to discharge their static – you must allow a few seconds for this to happen before you turn it on again. Should you turn it on again too soon, it may be that some of the information has not cleared properly but will be in an even more confused state now than it was before you shut it down. You can often hear static discharging inside the machine with little cracking and popping noises.

### Starting in safe mode
When a problem has occurred before shutting down Windows, your computer may restart itself in **safe mode**. This loads only the very basic drivers needed to start up your machine – it will disable additional drivers and settings. This allows you to remove or reset any offending problems that may have caused the errors in the first place, such as a wrongly configured display setting.

You can initialise safe mode yourself by restarting the computer and pressing the F8 key just as the 'Starting Windows 98' message appears. Your screen display may look totally different from how it usually does. This is because it starts up with the very basic 16 colours in the lowest resolution possible, so everything will look large and wishy-washy, but it will return to its old self when you start in normal mode again.

### Removing and reloading offending programs
When uninstalling a program, always use the uninstaller program if it

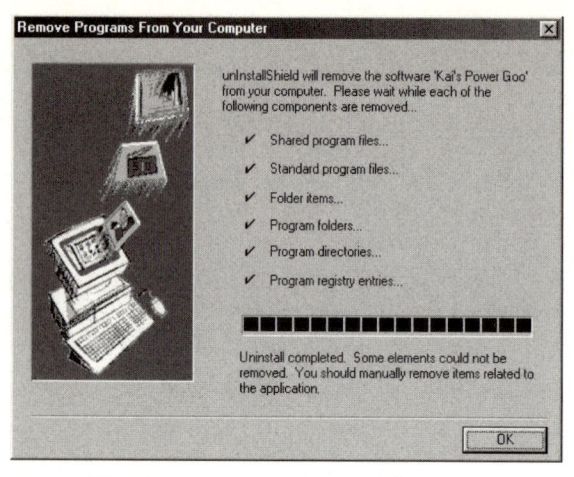

Fig. 105. The uninstall program shield.

has one. If not, go to the **Add/Remove Programs** in the **Control Panel** as discussed in Chapter 1 to see if it can be removed from there. The uninstaller program will ensure that all components are removed. If for any reason it cannot remove some components, it will advise you as shown in Figure 105. You can then check the folder in Explorer afterwards and manually remove any remnants.

*Should I remove shared files?*
If the uninstaller informs you that the program uses shared files and asks if you would like these removed as well, say **No**. Figure 106 shows an example of this question being asked. If a shared file is removed when another program also needs to use it, the other program will not work once it has gone.

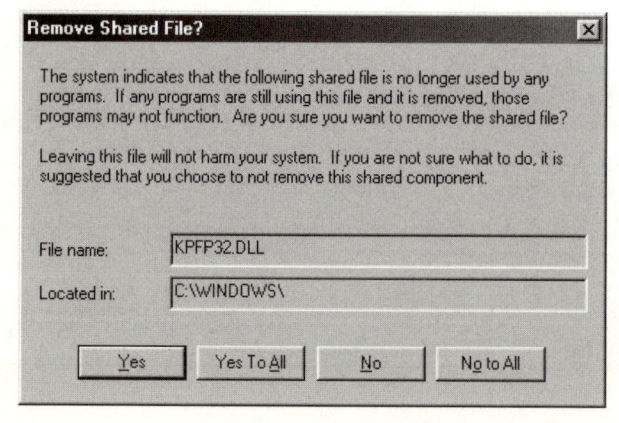

Fig. 106. Keeping shared files.

*Checking for the removal of a folder*
When a program has been uninstalled, then reinstalled, and it still throws up the same errors, you will need to uninstall it again and check that the original folder has been removed from the hard drive by looking in Explorer. With programs that create a personal user file such as IBM ViaVoice, the uninstaller will leave the file there. If it is this file that has corrupted the program, then whenever it is reinstalled it will keep throwing up the same errors until all references to this file have gone.

- **Uninstall** the program – keeping any shared files.
- Go into **Explorer** and click the **refresh** option from the **View** menu.
- Check for the **program folder** and any files that may have been left.
- Remove them by choosing to **delete**.
- **Hard reboot** the computer to ensure nothing related is being held in memory.
- **Reinstall** the program.

**Preventing errors from occurring**
Some good practices can be implemented which in turn can prevent errors from happening in the first place.

1. **Run the Defrag and Scandisk programs regularly**. This will keep your system clean and healthy. If any errors are becoming imminent on your hard drive, Scandisk will advise you of these. Defrag keeps your files neatly together and will advise of any lost fragments.

2. **Do not install programs that are of no use to you**. Installing all and sundry off the covers of magazines and demo disks will inevitably end up causing you problems sooner or later. These programs often have faults that can cause havoc with your computer. They can be a good way of trying a program before you buy it – but try one at a time with a period in between to make sure it hasn't caused your computer set-up any problems. If it does cause problems, you know which is the offending program or disk and can confine it to the place it deserves – the rubbish bin.

3. **Consider running a PC care program**. Utility programs such as **Norton Utilities**, **CrashGuard** and **First Aid** help to detect when your computer is having difficulties. Some attempt to halt your computer before a crash happens, giving you time to save your work;

others work by performing routines checks and diagnosis to prevent the crash happening in the first place.

4. **Take advantage of uninstall programs**. Whether you choose to use the program's own uninstaller, the Add/Remove Programs within Windows or a separate uninstaller utility such as Quarterdeck's **Clean Sweep**, proper removing of programs will help to prevent errors occurring by removing references to the uninstalled programs from all of the Windows system files.

## IT'S NOT ALWAYS THE FAULT OF THE OBVIOUS

People often blame computers – how many times have you rung a company about a problem and been given the excuse 'it's the computers fault'? It often isn't the computer that has caused the fault at all, more likely either the operator or the software. Computers need to be given specific instructions, everything has to be just so – they haven't got a mind of their own. You tell a computer to do something and it will do it, but if you don't do your bit it gets confused and errors occur.

*Computer versus operators theory*
The operating system is the language translator between you and the computer. You tell the computer what to do via the mouse and keyboard through menu systems and toolbars. The program along with the operating system convert these instructions into a language the computer can understand and off it goes. It takes these instructions literally – it cannot differentiate between what you say you want and what you may really want. If you try to do something that isn't allowed, or the program needs to do something that the computer isn't set up for, all will not go to plan.

We will now explain some simple problems that have simple solutions but may be far from obvious – until you understand this theory. Remember that computers can't read minds and don't have a sense of humour!

### Problem number one
Mary has a word processor that is **WYSIWYG** ('what you see is what you get'). This means that what she sees on the screen should be what it will look like when it is printed. She designs a small notice for her office door as seen on the left side of Figure 107. When it is printed it comes out like the right side of Figure 107.

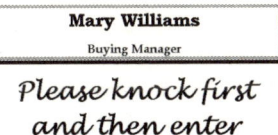

| Mary Williams | Mary Williams |
|---|---|
| Buying Manager | Buying Manager |
| *Please knock first and then enter* | **Please knock first and then enter** |

Fig. 107. The effect of an incorrect printer driver.

*Operator's diagnosis*
There must be something wrong with her word processor – everything she prints is coming out wrong. She tries a different program and that does the same – printing out totally differently from how it displayed on the screen. Her friend has got the same printer, so she tries swapping printers but the result is no different, so it can't be that.

*Real diagnosis*
Mary has the **wrong printer driver** loaded. A driver translates instructions between the program and the peripheral. The driver is converting the instructions as if it is printing to a Hewlett Packard 400 printer, when it is in fact a Hewlett Packard 550 printer.

**Problem number two**
Robert has just bought a new scanner. He plugs it in, loads the drivers and scans his favourite photograph. When he goes to print it out, his computer tells him his printer is out of paper. It isn't – there's plenty of paper there.

*Operator's diagnosis*
It can't be the scanner because it scans fine. His printer worked alright before. It is the type of scanner that plugs into the parallel port of his computer and the printer plugs into the back of the scanner. The through port that connects the printer must be at fault or the printer and scanner must be conflicting with each other.

*Real diagnosis*
When **two peripherals use the same port** as in this instance, it may not be possible to use both at the same time. The scanned photograph needs to be transferred into a photo-editing package such as Paint Shop Pro so that the scanner program can be shut down, thus freeing up the port. The printer will then be operational again.

### Problem number three

After loading a new game the sound doesn't work properly. It sounds as if you are firing something from a machine gun. The last game Philip loaded was the same and he gave up with that – but now he's convinced there is something wrong with his computer.

*Operator's diagnosis*
It has happened on two games now – it has got to be his sound card that is at fault.

*Real diagnosis*
Philip does not understand the **sound set-up** files. He has been loading the games with Sound Blaster Pro configuration settings when his sound card is only Sound Blaster Compatible. He has gone along with the settings the manufacturer suggests because this has always worked with previous programs (they didn't have sound!). This time it didn't – his computer has a sound set-up IRQ of 5, when the manufacturer suggested 7 as seen in Figure 108 on the left side. We discovered this by checking out the resources from **Device Manager** as seen on the right side of Figure 108.

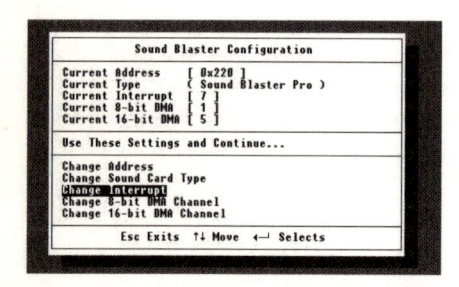

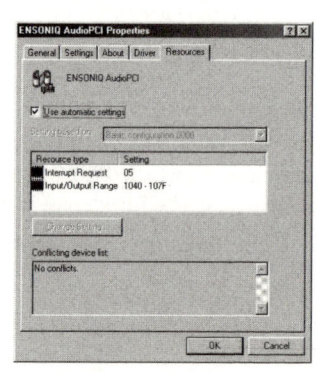

Fig. 108. Reading sound configurations.

### Problem number four
Every time Sharon starts her computer it runs the Scandisk program.

*Operator diagnosis*
There is something wrong with her computer.

*Real diagnosis*
Sharon is not shutting Windows down using the correct procedure.

Selecting **Shut Down** from the menu and allowing the computer time to save all changed files ready for the next time she uses her computer is what the system expects to happen. Sharon has been selecting **Shut Down** from the Start menu and just turning off the power before waiting for the screen that says it is now safe to turn off your computer.

### Problem number five
Barry is using Windows 95. He has just loaded a program that didn't put anything in the menu system. He wants to put a shortcut on the desktop so went to Explorer to find the .exe file. He cannot find the folder that contains the file.

*Operator's diagnosis*
He has not loaded the program properly and attempts it again. The same thing happened, so he loads it yet again but in a different folder. No success. The CD is at fault.

*Real diagnosis*
Explorer is not automatically refreshing his view of the folders on his hard drive. From the View menu, choosing to **Refresh** the tree reveals the missing folders.

### Problem number six
Rachel has been downloading some photographs from her digital camera. She said she had to unplug her mouse to be able to plug the camera into the back of her computer. She has now plugged her mouse back in but it isn't working.

*Operator's diagnosis*
She thinks she has broken her mouse and may need a new one.

*Real diagnosis*
Windows loads the mouse driver on boot up. Because she unplugged it and used the port for downloading photographs, Windows now doesn't realise she has her mouse back again. Restarting Windows solves the problem.
    Rachel could have used the other port, COM 2, for her camera. If it has a different connection plug, an adapter can be purchased very cheaply to convert the plug.

### Problem number seven
James has bought a second-hand computer for his college work. He

cannot get the program to enter a pound sign on his accounting sheets. Every time he presses the shift-3 key on his keyboard for the £ sign, he gets the # sign.

*Operator's diagnosis*
There is something wrong with the keyboard – he thinks he will have to buy a new one.

*Real diagnosis*
His computer is set up for an American keyboard. By going into **Control Panel** and selecting the **keyboard** icon, he can change the language to UK English as shown in Figure 109. He would be well advised to check the **Regional Settings** in the Control Panel as well – if this is also set to American English it may affect the way dates are displayed.

This is a point to bear in mind when installing any software. Much of it is American based and may have to be told that you are working with an English (British) keyboard, want to use an English (British) spell checker and dictionary and want to use English (European) paper measurements such as A4 as standard, not English (American).

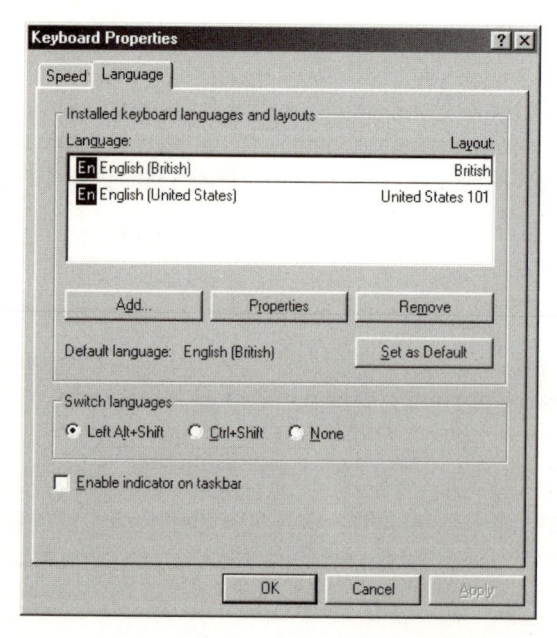

Fig. 109. Setting the correct keyboard.

## Problem number eight
Daniel wants to use his joystick to play a game, but it isn't working.

*Operator's diagnosis*
The joystick is faulty.

*Real diagnosis*
Joysticks are plugged into the **games port** on a **sound card**. This port was disabled on Daniel's sound card. Checking the manual that came with his sound card revealed a jumper setting that needed changing to re-enable it. His joystick was then working but needed calibrating in the **Joysticks** section of the **Control Panel** in order to work correctly.

## SUMMARY

Running **Scandisk** and **Defrag** regularly, together with ensuring the correct installation and removal of software and hardware, will help you to avoid most problems. Occasionally even the most careful of users will nonetheless experience problems, and when this happens to you, try to remember the following:

- Think logically – what were you doing immediately prior to the problem occurring?
- Backtrack carefully – what have you installed or removed recently?
- When did it last work properly – what has happened since?
- Try to narrow the problem down – write down all error messages.
- If you try to correct it, try one thing at a time and make a note of your steps.
- Don't forget to try a hard reboot – you won't harm the machine and it's surprising how often this will work.
- After a hard reboot, can you make the fault happen again?
- Last, but not least, don't pull anything to bits just to see how it works and don't try fixing something that isn't broken.

# Appendix
## Recommended Software and Hardware Purchases

There are so many programs available that it can be confusing to know what package is required for which job. We suggest the following programs as easy to use, and good value for money. All are available from popular computer software outlets such as Electronic Boutique, PC World or one of the many mail order computer software outlets.

**Microsoft Office (Small Business Edition).** Incorporates Word (word processor), Excel (spreadsheet), Outlook (information manager), Publisher (desktop publisher) and Autoroute (car route planner). An excellent suite of programs that will enable the user to perform most routine computer tasks. Its full retail price is around £300. This can be reduced to around £100 if it is purchased at the same time as a new computer, or if there is a student member within the household. Many schools use this program for their curriculum work.

**Microsoft Works**. Incorporates a word processor, spreadsheet and very easy-to-use database. Has many wizard templates and represents excellent value for money at less than £50.

**Paint Shop Pro by Jasc software**. A comprehensive photo-editing package. Scanning can be performed from directly within the program. Controls are easy to use and understand in a short time. Creates and edits all kinds of images, takes screen captures and performs graphic file conversions. A 30-day evaluation copy can often be found on the cover-disk of computer magazines or can be downloaded from **www.shareware.com**. Retails at around £50.

**Quicken by Intuit**. A money program ideally suited to home finance. Very easy to set up and use with provision for future planning goals and home inventory lists in the deluxe version. Particularly good for automated deductions such as direct debits, etc. Standard version costs around £25, whereas the deluxe version is around £45.

**For Your Eyes Only by Symantec Norton**. A security program that works by the encryption of files. Allows one Super User who controls all aspects and any number of secondary users, each having their own encryption options. Around £50.

**Winzip by Nico Mac Computing Inc**. An excellent file compression program. Allows you to add and update files inside the main zip file and to extract copies of individual files. Has the facility to span large files over multiple floppy disks. The shareware version is most often listed within the utility or Internet tool sections of magazine coverdisks or is available direct from the company's web site at **http://www.winzip.com** for $29.

**Symantec Norton Anti-Virus.** Protects your computer from viruses. Immediately halts any virus being transferred from the Internet, a floppy disk, CD-ROM, macro or e-mail. Has the ability to send captured viruses to head office for analysis. Retails for around £25.

**Partition Magic by PowerQuest**. Allows multiple operating systems to be run on one computer. Creates separate partitions for data file backups and can restructure cluster sizes to gain wasted space. Around £40.

**PC Anywhere by Norton**. Allows remote control of your PC via a modem. Connect your home PC with the office or connect from your mobile. Easy and quick to use with good security measures. Around £60.

## FOR THOSE TIMES WHEN YOU DESERVE A LITTLE LEISURE.

**Combat Flight Simulator by Microsoft**. Feels just like the real thing – Second World War version of the original flight simulator. Battle it out either against the computer or over a network with a friend. Approx. £35.

**Colin McRae Rally**. A realistic car rally game with time trials, rallies and training school sessions. Play against computer team members or against a friend over the network. £30.

**Duke Nukem Forever**. Part of the Duke series that wasn't out when this book was going to press. The rest of the series are excellent shoot-em-up strategy games and we are sure this will follow suit. Once again, play against the computer or with a friend over the network.

## RECOMMENDED HARDWARE THAT IS REFERRED TO IN THIS BOOK AND ACTUALLY USED BY THE AUTHORS.

**Computer from Evesham Micros**. Supplier of good build quality machines at realistic prices. They have the 'extras' available for those who want them, but do not include them all as the 'norm'. A two-year on-site warranty is part of the price.
Evesham Micros Ltd, Vale Park, Evesham WR11 6TD.
Tel: 01386 769790. Web site: **http://www.evesham.com**.

**Monitor from Taxan**. Good quality monitors and excellent aftersales service. Available from some good computer outlets or from:
Taxan (Europe) Ltd., Taxan House, Cookham Road, Bracknell, Berks RG12 1RB.
Tel: 01344 484646. Web site: **http://www.taxan.co.uk**.

**Digital Camera by Ricoh**. Good quality sturdy camera with many features including being able to take sound files as well as stills. For a mid-range camera it does a top range job. Available at good camera shops. Web site: **http://www.ricoh.com**.

**ActionTec Memory Card Reader**. Enables fast transfer of photo files from digital camera sim card to computer without the need for 'downloading'. Available from good camera shops.
Web site: **http://www.actiontec.com**.

**Flatbed Scanner from Black Widow**. Produces a good quality scan and has easy-to-use controls. Prices on a par with other lesser quality scanners. Devcom International Ltd., Devcom House, Winchester Avenue, Denny FK6 6QE.
Tel: 01324 825999. Web site: **http://www.blackwidow.co.uk**.

**Colour Printer from Epson**. Good bright colours and excellent print speed. Easy paper loading and cartridge-changing methods. Facility to use high resolution printing on special glossy paper.
Epson UK Ltd., Campus 100, Maylands Avenue, Hemel Hempstead, Herts HP2 7TJ.
Tel: 01442 61144.

# Glossary

**Accessibility.** A number of options available within Windows to enable greater ease of use for those with disabilities.

**BMP.** BitMap Paint, a graphic file format traditionally used by Windows. It is widely recognised by other software packages but files tend to be on the large side.

**Backup.** A Microsoft program included with all versions of Windows, which can be used to store copies of files to another disk or medium in case of loss or damage to the originals.

**Bootable start-up disk.** Usually a floppy disk that contains a copy of the computer's system files. It can be used to start the computer in an emergency where the hard disk files have become unstable.

**Bullet.** A shape, number or letter used, normally within a word processor, to add emphasis or interest to a list of points.

**CD writer.** A CD drive that is capable of recording data onto CD-ROM disks. A CD Re-Writer is capable of using CD-RW disks. Blank CR-RW disks are much more expensive than CD-ROMs but can be used more than once.

**Cloning.** A method of producing an exact copy of something. A cloning tool is normally found within a photo-editing package and used to copy areas of a photo.

**Communications.** One computer exchanging data with another in some way. See also **Network**.

**Control Palette.** A dialogue box that enables the user of an image editing package to alter the properties of a particular tool such as its size or shape.

**Control panel.** A window within Windows, found on the start menu/ settings. It gives access to features, which enable alteration of the properties of some software and hardware.

**Cut and paste.** A term used in the printing industry describing the action of cutting out areas of type and pictures, and then sticking them on a blank piece of paper to make up the page of a magazine/newspaper etc. This is now carried out electronically within a computer program.

**Database.** This is a program which is used to store information that may be retrieved in a manner that is beneficial to the user.

**Defrag.** Also known as a disk defragmentation program. This utility scans a disk looking for files that have become broken up into fragments. Such files will be reassembled in the correct order so that they may be accessed more quickly.

**Desktop publishing.** The production of a magazine, book, flyer, etc. using text and/or pictures for later printing.

**Desktop theme.** A grouping consisting of wallpaper, sounds, cursors and events that add interest to your desktop and which enable the user to personalise their computer.

**Dial-up networking.** A method of linking two computers together so that they may share or exchange data using modems and a telephone line.

**Digital camera.** Similar to a normal camera but which instead of using film, stores its images on a small memory chip that slots inside the camera body.

**Direct cable connection.** When two computers that are next to each other are connected via their parallel or serial ports using a null modem cable.

**Disk image.** A file that contains a 'snapshot' of the contents of a disk drive at a particular moment in time. Such a file would be used to restore the structure of a hard disk following a disaster such as serious corruption of files or the operating system.

**Download (Internet).** The process of copying a program or file from a site on the web to your own computer for later use.

**Download (photographs).** The process of copying the image files from the memory card of a digital camera to your computer.

**Encryption.** The adding of a code to a saved file or program, which makes it unusable without the correct password. This is a powerful security feature, which prevents unauthorised personnel from using, copying or deleting files to which they are not entitled to have access.

**Fatal exception.** Something within the computer has tried to do something that it shouldn't or can't. There is nothing that can be done to retrieve this . You may be lucky and clear the problem by turning your computer off and waiting a minute or two before turning it back on. If it doesn't work contact your computer manufacturer's support line or your engineer.

**File sharing.** This must be enabled through 'My Computer' or 'Explorer' in order to allow access to others using a **network** or **direct cable connection**. This generally applies to the computer acting as the 'host'.

**Fill series.** A term used within a **spreadsheet** meaning to generate automatically the next relative data entry and enter it in the next data field. This is commonly used to complete a list of days, months or a series of required numbers.

**Font.** A font is a typeface alphabet of a particular design as used in a program such as a word processor. There are many thousands available, enabling documents to be prepared in eye-catching and attractive ways.

**Frozen screen.** This is where, no matter what you do, you can do nothing. Your mouse may still move around but its buttons and the keys on the keyboard will produce no response. Most of the time pressing the Ctrl, Alt and Delete keys simultaneously will enable you to shut down the program that has stopped responding. If not, a **hard reboot** will usually solve the problem.

**General protection fault.** This is similar to the **fatal exception** error though generally not so serious. If this occurs it will normally be accompanied by a message telling you that the program will be closed and any unsaved work will be lost. Providing that you have been saving your work regularly this will cause only minimum inconvenience.

**Gif.** Graphic interchange format. Another type of file format used to save graphical information. Images saved in this format are of reduced size since they can display only 256 colours. Frequently used for web pages.

**Graphics.** A term used to describe any image that appears on the computer screen that is not editable text.

**Guest.** The term used to refer to a computer that is being linked to another, known as the **host**, in order that it may utilise the host's resources or files.

**Handshaking.** When two computers attempt to connect they exchange codes to ensure they are both compatible. It's a form of introducing themselves and hence the term.

**Hard reboot.** Restarting the computer after switching off the power to the machine. A hard reboot will clear any memory resident programs.

**Host.** This is the name given to a computer which is sharing its resources or files with a **guest**.

**Hyperlink.** A word or phrase in a contrasting colour usually found in a web page or e-mail. When clicked on, the hyperlink will take the readers to a related topic. This could be within the same document or to a completely different site.

**Illegal functions.** An error message usually seen as part of a **general protection fault**, although it can also appear on its own. Displayed when a program tries to access memory resources which are unavailable to it.

**Import.** This is the copying of a file into another file, e.g. when you place a graphic into a word-processor document.

**Index file.** The first page of a web site.

**Install.** This can refer to either the fitting of a piece of hardware, or the setting up of a piece of software to run from the fixed disk.

**Internet.** A global network of computers that allow the free exchange of information between them. Anyone may access this network by using a special high-speed digital telephone line (ISDN) or an Internet Service Provider (ISP).

**Jpeg.** Joint Photographic Experts Group. Another graphic format which records graphics files in a compressed format offering greatly reduced file sizes. Commonly used by digital cameras to record photographs, and for transmission of graphics via e-mail, etc.

**Lasso.** A tool used in graphics editing which enables the selection of irregularly shaped objects or areas of a photograph.

**Macro.** A collection of keystroke instructions linked together to perform a shortcut actuated by pressing one or two keys simultaneously. This would be mainly used to perform common actions with a single keystroke instead of having to navigate through a series of menus.

**Mail merge.** This is a useful function that allows a single letter to be typed with tokens inserted where certain information should be placed. Each copy of the letter that is printed can automatically extract the required information from within a given database. This means that each copy of the letter can be different and personalised.

**Map a drive.** Drive mapping is the practice of one computer on a **network** allocating one of its drive letters to a resource on another machine. This would enable the user of the machine containing the mapped drives to see the resources of other machines as if they were a drive on their machine.

**Merging cells.** This is a feature of a **spreadsheet** that allows several adjoining cells to be treated as a single cell.

**Network.** Two or more computers that are connected together in some way so that they can communicate with each other and share information and/or resources.

**Network neighbourhood.** Part of Windows that enables those connected to a **network** to see who else is connected and what resources are available.

**OCR.** Optical Character Recognition is the use of a **scanner** to 'read' a piece of printed text and convert it from a graphic to a document that can be edited with a word processor.

**Partitions.** A hard drive may be divided into two or more sections for a variety of reasons. Each section is known as a partition.

**Reboot.** Rebooting a computer just means to restart it. This can be a soft reboot performed by using the reset button on the computer or by pressing the Ctrl, Alt and Delete keys simultaneously, or a **hard reboot** which involves shutting the machine down completely and turning off the power for a short while.

**Resolution.** This usually refers to the number of pixels, or dots, per inch that makes up an image. The higher the number of these dots, the finer the quality of the image.

**Safe mode.** A basic configuration of Windows which will load if a normal start-up has been unsuccessful. No device drivers will be loaded and the CD-ROM will not normally be available. This mode simply allows you to correct any faults –hopefully – and back up any files.

**Scandisk.** One of the system tools included with Windows that will check a disk for a variety of errors. It has the ability to correct simple problems and save corrupted data as a separate file. Such files are of little or no use to the home user but may contain data valuable for an engineer if the problem persists.

**Scanner.** A device, similar to a photocopier, for copying printed material and saving it as a graphic for later use by the computer.

**Search engine.** A utility found on the **Internet** that can search its databases for any reference to the topics entered by the user. It will then supply links and addresses for further searches thus assisting the enquirer to locate the information they require. There are many search engines available on the net such as Lycos, Yahoo! and AltaVista.

**Spreadsheet.** A program that enables calculations to be performed using data and formulae placed in boxes called cells. The results can then be used to produce graphs and charts for inclusion in reports, etc. Spreadsheets will recalculate all equations if any data is changed, making them very powerful 'What if?' tools.

**Tab order.** The order in which pressing the tab key moves the cursor around the fields in a **database**.

**Tabs (WP).** Tabs in a word processor are set in much the same way as on a typewriter but in a word processor produce fixed points to which the cursor will jump when the tab key is pressed.

**Taskbar.** The narrow strip at the bottom of the screen in Windows 95/98 that tells you what programs are open and may also contain shortcut icons for frequently used programs. The taskbar can be repositioned to any edge of the screen simply by dragging it around.

**TIF.** Tagged Image Format. Yet another graphic file extension mainly used in **desktop publishing** but not as popular as it once was. This file format is not a standard and a program may read one TIF but not another – this may lead to its demise.

**Uninstall.** To remove a program from a fixed disk along with files that the original install program placed in folders such as Windows System and Registry. Also known as a clean removal.

**URL.** Uniform Resource Locator. The technical name for the address of a web site.

**Word processing.** A method of producing letters and other documents electronically using a computer or specialised machine. Word-processed documents can contain many fonts, styles and sizes of letter and may be held on a data medium for later printing. A vast improvement on the typewriter, and cheaper on paper.

**World Wide Web.** A world-wide network of computers linking databases that share information with each other. Such networks can be accessed via an ISP or by using a dedicated ISDN line.

**Zip drive.** A high capacity drive that uses disks similar in appearance to a thick floppy. Useful for backing up large amounts of data, storing archived files or disk imaging. Very cost effective and relatively quick.

**Zip file.** A file which has been compressed using a utility program such as WinZip.

# Further Reading

### ESSENTIALS

*1000 Best Web Sites*, Bruce Durie, How To Books, 1999. £9.99. This invaluable guide takes you straight to the best sites without that frustrating, time-consuming (and sometimes fruitless) searching.

*ComputerActive*. VNU Publications. A fortnightly magazine that has much essential reading including workshops of a variety of everyday tasks that can be completed on the computer. 99p from most newsagents on alternate Thursdays.

*Getting Started on the Internet*, Irene Krechnowiecka, published by How To Books Ltd, 1999. £5. from most bookshops. From How To Books' *Essentials* series, an invaluable and accessible guide for first-time users of the Internet.

*The Internet – The Rough Guide*. Angus J. Kennedy. A direct and to-the-point guide to what all the fuss is about, along with hundreds of web site addresses in a convenient category-type listing. £5.99 from most bookshops and PC World.

### MICROSOFT OFFICE PRODUCTS

There are many other good books available to enable you to increase your knowledge in a particular area. Some that we have seen and can recommend are listed below. Books are expensive so before you buy please do ensure it covers the subject you wish to improve and in particular that it covers the version of the program you have on your computer.

Que Publishing produce a complete range of books which cover all aspects of Microsoft Office. These are either as the **6in1** range that includes a section on all programs in the Office suite, or the **Using** range where each one specialises on just one of the programs in Microsoft Office. They are all excellent books.

*Microsoft Office 97 (Small Business Edition)*. Classified as a new to casual reader level, this book covers all six elements of the small business edition of this classic Microsoft suite. £27.49. ISBN 0-7897-1352-7.

*Microsoft Office 97 (Professional Edition)*, Faithe Wempen. As above but including Powerpoint and Access instead of Publisher and Autoroute. £27.49. ISBN 0-7897-1515-5.

*Using Microsoft Word 97*, Bill Carnarda. A more in-depth look at this industry standard word processor. £32.99. ISBN 0-7897-1398-5.

*Using Excel 97.* A step-by-step walkthrough explaining the complexities of involved spreadsheet work. £37.49. ISBN 0-7897-1399-3.

The web site for Que can be found at **http://www.quecorp.com**

*Access in Easy Steps*, Stephen Copestake. £7.50. Will help you through the basic problems encountered when using this database for the first time. ISBN 1-874029-78-4. Web site at **http://www.computerstep.com**.

## OTHER SPECIALIST SUBJECTS

*Networking – in Easy Steps,* Peter Ingram. An ideal beginners' book for learning more about the different ways of connecting two computers together. £8.99. ISBN 1-874029-92-X. Web site at **http://www.computerstep.com**.

*Teach Yourself Paint Shop Pro 5 in 24 Hours.* T. Michael Clark, Sams Publishing. Takes the reader through all the common aspects of this image-editing package. £17.95. ISBN 0-672-31362-6. Web site: **http://www.samspublishing.com**.

*Digital Photography Answers*, Dave Johnson. A very good book that explains this sometimes complex subject very well. ISBN 0-07-211884-9. £22.99. Web site http://www.osborne.com.

*Windows 98 Answers*, Martin S. Matthews and Carole Boggs Matthews, Osborne. A superb book for the curious who wish to become intermediate users of Windows. £23.99. ISBN 0-07-882455-9.

*Carol Vorderman's Guide to the Internet*. Clear explanations of typical questions on this subject. £9.99. ISBN 0-13-079983-1.

# Index

accessibility options, 17
accounts, 81
add new hardware, 16
Add/Remove Programs, 14
adding/removing fields (DB), 95
adding/removing Windows
  components, 14
address book, creating (DB), 93
addresses on the Internet, 105
ascending order (SS), 71

backup, 23
balancing accounts, 83, 87
BMP, 38
bootable startup disk, 16
borders and lines (SS), 69
building a web page, 112
bullets (WP), 56

CD writers, 128
cell size, 66
charts (SS), 72
chronological ordering (SS), 70
cloning, 43
column width, 67
columns and tables (WP), 48
combo box, 77
communications, 134
connecting to the Internet, 103
control palette, 45
Control Panel, 13
creating drawings and pictures
  (WP), 52
creating partitions, 129
cut and pasting, 40

databases, 91
date and time icon, 16
defrag, 153
descending order (SS), 71
desktop themes, 19
dial-up networking, 140
digital camera, 34, 157

direct cable connection, 28
direct debit payments, 82
disk imaging, 131
downloading (Internet), 109
downloading photographs, 36

e-mail address, 104
encryption, 120
entertainment menu, 24
errors, 146

fatal exception, 148
field (DB), 92
file sharing, 137
file types and conversions (WP), 61
fill series, 70
finance programs, 81
finding lost files, 22
fonts, 20
frozen screens, 149
FTP site, 110

general protection faults, 148
gif, 38
graphics, 38
gridlines (SS), 75
grouping objects (WP), 53
guesting a network, 30, 143

handshaking, 136
hard reboot, 150
hosting a network, 29, 142
hyperlink, 105, 115

identity on the web, 103
illegal function, 148
importing and exporting (WP), 61
income and outgoings, 88
index file, 112
inserting pictures (WP), 54
installing and removing programs, 14
installing and viewing fonts, 20
Internet, 103

Internet address, 105

jpeg, 38

keyboard properties, 17, 158

labels, producing and printing (DB), 92, 99
language setup, 17
lasso, 41

macros (WP), 59
magnifying selections, 18
mail merge, 92, 100
manipulating photographs, 40
mapping a drive, 138
marking records (DB), 99
media player, 25
merging cells, 68
missing files, 146
money programs, 81
mouse freezes, 149
multimedia, 25
music CDs, 27

network cards and configurations, 135
Network Neighbourhood, 30, 138
network properties, 29, 134
numbering (WP), 57

OCR (optical character recognition), 58

Paint Shop Pro, 35
partition addresses, 129
photographs, 34
playing sound and video, 25, 26, 156
printer, 35
printer sharing, 137
printing charts (SS), 74
problems, 145
publishing a web page, 116

questions and queries (DB), 98
quick fill cells, 70

reboot, 150

recording sound files, 31
recovery disks, 131
removing programs, 147
resolution, 38
restart, 146
restricting use, 120
row height, 67

safe mode, 151
scandisk, 153, 157
scanner, 35, 155
scanning text (OCR), 58
search engines, 106, 117
security programs, 120
smart edge, 42
soft reboot, 150
sorting records (DB), 98
sound recorder, 26
spanning, 126
spreadsheets, 66

tab order (DB), 97
tables and columns (WP), 48
tabs (WP), 55
taskbar properties, 22
ten base (10BASE2), 135
tif, 38
tracking money, 82

uninstalling programs, 14, 151
unzipping, 123
uploading, 116
URLs, 106
usernames, 104

voice dictation, 58

web space, 112
Windows setup, 15
WinZip, 123
word processing, 48
World Wide Web (WWW), 103
wrapping (WP), 54
Yahoo!, 108

Zip drives, 127
zip files, 122

## 1000 BEST WEB SITES
**Access the most useful sites around**

Bruce Durie

Finding the right web site can be costly both in time and money. Not any more! This invaluable guide takes you straight to the best sites without that frustrating, time-consuming (and sometimes fruitless) searching. Whatever your interest, you'll find the best sites here. Sites that are attractive, quick to load and full of interest. They're easy to read, full of exciting links that actually do work, and they have that certain something that makes you want to revisit them time and time again. Bruce Durie is a well-known author and broadcaster. He works at Napier University, Edinburgh, mostly on e-business and online learning projects. He has also written *Creating a Web Site* in the How To Series.

*216pp 1 85703 540 2*


## GETTING STARTED ON THE INTERNET
**Access a world of information**

Irene Krechowiecka

If you don't know your ISP from your browser, or your POP account from your modem … this is the book for you. Get on-line for the least money and in the shortest time. Discover how to use email, join in newsgroup discussions and access information from around the world. Whether you want to investigate health issues, plan the perfect holiday, or check the latest share prices, the Internet has something for you! Irene Krechowiecka has written a number of books on the practical use of the internet. And she runs courses for beginners on using this remarkable resource.

*83pp 1 85703 516 X*

**Some other useful titles from How To Books**

**BUYING A PERSONAL COMPUTER**
**How to specify, select and buy your ideal PC**

Allen Brown

Many thousands of personal computers (PCs) are sold annually and they are becoming general purpose, everyday tools. Buying a PC for the first time represents a significant financial outlay. This book, now in an updated fourth edition, will help potential buyers in their choice of PC, their selection of peripherals, and appropriate software. It aims so be precise, yet with sufficient information to enable a new user to understand a PC specification and to ensure that it will be adequate for their needs. It will also provide information on applications that the buyer may be thinking of for the future. Dr Allen Brown is a Senior Lecturer in Electronics in the School of Applied Sciences at Anglia Polytechnic University, Cambridge.

*176pp illus. 1 85703 547 X 4th edition*


**CREATING A WEB SITE**
**How to build a web site in a weekend and keep it in good shape**

Bruce Durie

Anyone can have a web site and anyone can design one – you don't have to be a computer wizard. All you need is a standard multimedia PC, a modem, some basic software, a few good ideas, a design and some free time. Whether you want your own home page, a site for your school, club, church or group, small business or major company, this step-by-step book gives you the know-how to create your own web site.

*144pp illus. 1 85703 356 6*

## USING THE INTERNET
**How to make the most of the information superhighway**

Graham Jones

Soon, nearly everyone in the developed world will have access to the Internet. This down-to-earth book, now in its second edition, shows you how and where to begin. Unlike many other books on the 'Net', this practical guide will really help you get onto the Net and start exploring the new 'information superhighway'.

*128pp   illus.   1 85703 237 3.  2nd edition*


## MAKING A WEDDING SPEECH
**How to prepare and deliver a confident and memorable address**

John Bowden

At thousands of weddings each year, many people are called on to 'say a few words'. But what DO you say? How do you find the right words which will go down really well with the assembled company? Written by an experienced public speaker, this entertaining book shows you how to put together a simple but effective speech. Whether you are the best man, bridegroom, father of the bride or other participant, you'll find help at all stages: from great opening lines to apt quotations, anecdotes, tips on using humour, together with 50 short model speeches which you can use or adapt. 'Invest in a copy ... packed with opening lines, jokes and model speeches.' *Brides Magazine*. This popular book is now in its fourth edition.

*166pp.   illus.   1 85703 385 X.  4th edition*

**176** Some other useful titles from How To Books

## LEARNING TO READ MUSIC
**How to make sense of those mysterious symbols**

Peter Nickol

Would you like to revive your guitar, flute or piano-playing? Or is your child learning an instrument and you'd like to be able help? Perhaps you sing in a choir and your music-reading is a bit shaky. Whatever your reason, if you would like to make sense of all those mysterious musical symbols, this book will explain what they mean, in simple, easy-to-understand terms. In straightforward stages you can learn about pitch, rhythm, keys and much more. Peter Nickol is an award-winning music book editor, who has worked on many books widely used in schools.

*111pp illus. 1 85703 390 6*


## BUYING A HOUSE
**How to find, choose and pay for your own home**

Adam Walker

This book is a practical guide to buying your own home. It explains clearly every stage of the process and gives an expert's view on how to avoid all the most common pitfalls. It will show you how to decide between renting and buying, how to get the best out of estate agents, how to choose the right property, assess its value and negotiate the best purchase price, and how to choose the right mortgage and get the sale through to a swift and satisfactory conclusion. Adam Walker is a management consultant, broadcaster and journalist who has specialised in the residential property market for more than 15 years. He is a regular contributor to *The Sunday Times*, *House Beautiful Magazine*, GMTV, BBC Radio 2 and Talk Radio.

*144pp illus. 1 85703 292 6*